Y0-DYS-524

SHANGHAI

East
China
Sea

I   N   A

CHUNGKING   River

Yangtze

TAIPEI

TAIWAN

CANTON

HONG KONG

HANOI

HAIPHONG

AOS

IANE

Mekong   River

NORTH VIETNAM
17° 1954 DEMARCATION
LINE

MANILA

P
H
I
L
I
P
P
I
N
E
S

LAND

SOUTH
VIETNAM

South   China   Sea

8

HNOM PENH

SAIGON

Gulf of

CAMBODIA

MALAYSIA

BRUNEI

KUALA LUMPUR

SINGAPORE

BORNEO

N   D   O   N   E   S   I   A

Hal Dareff is editor-in-chief of juvenile and young adult books for a New York publisher, and has been a special projects editor for Parents' Magazine Press, a contributing editor to *Parents' Magazine*, and editor of *Children's Digest*. He has written many magazine articles and is the author of several books, including MAN IN ORBIT, THE FIRST MICROSCOPE, and JACQUELINE KENNEDY, A PORTRAIT IN COURAGE. Born in New York City in 1920, he attended Washington and Lee University and The New School for Social Research. He lives in Westport, Connecticut with his wife and two sons. The cover design and illustration is by Charles and Cuffari.

THE STORY OF VIETNAM

Hal Dareff

AN AVON CAMELOT book

AVON BOOKS
A division of
The Hearst Corporation
959 Eighth Avenue
New York, New York 10019

First Printing Camelot Edition, November, 1967
Second Printing, May, 1968

CAMELOT TRADEMARK REG. U.S. PAT. OFF. AND
FOREIGN COUNTRIES, REGISTERED TRADEMARK—
MARCA REGISTRADA, HECHO EN CHICAGO, U.S.A.

Printed in the U.S.A.

To my friend and colleague,
Harold Schwartz, whose idea it was

Contents

Introduction   11

Author's Note   13

1. People of the Red River   17
2. Threat from the West   32
3. The March of Conquest   41
4. French Indochina   54
5. Communism and Ho Chi Minh   67
6. End of an Empire   80
7. The Americans and the Mandarin   96
8. Guerrilla War and the Viet Cong   113
9. The Decline and Fall of Ngo Dinh Diem   126
10. An American War   146

Index   169

VIETNAM
and neighboring countries

SCALE OF MILES
0   50   100   150

INTRODUCTION

By Professor Richard I. Miller

Author of *Teaching About Communism, Dag Hammarskjold and Crisis Diplomacy,* and *Perspectives on Educational Change.* Consultant to the National Education Association and the U.S. Office of Education. At the University of Kentucky, Dr. Miller is Director of the Program on Educational Change and a member of the graduate faculty in the College of Education.

I am pleased to write this introduction for several reasons, but for two in particular. *The Story of Vietnam* by Hal Dareff is an unusually fine book in terms of its purpose, and in its success at combining sound scholarship and readability—no easy feat. It should reach and hold the attention of young people in a way rarely achieved on so difficult and vital a subject. Secondly, the book is important because it indicates an awakening interest by publishers in books for young readers that will deal realistically with world affairs.

Not too long ago, lands as distant and remote as Vietnam had little meaning for Americans. Contemporary events, however, have shown that even a small country may hold the key to the fate of great nations. This is a valuable lesson to have learned, for the crisis in Vietnam is surely not the last problem we will have to face in our times.

Keeping this in mind, it is esential that the education of

our young people in these matters not be neglected. This education cannot begin at too early an age. The elementary years and beyond should provide a firm foundation of knowledge and understanding about some of the world's more basic problems. Politics and international affairs can be meaningful and exciting if they are taught or written about by those who are deeply informed and know how to communicate facts and ideas to young people.

Mr. Dareff's book makes an important contribution in this area. Any reader, young or old, will find it, as I did, a reliable guide to the early history of Vietnam and to the complexities of its recent history.

The publishers are to be commended for launching this new *Background Books* series. *The Story of Vietnam* sets a high standard for future volumes.

AUTHOR'S NOTE

My objectives in writing this book were threefold. One was to relate the story of Vietnam's past, which has been a remarkable one. Another was to show how the impact of Europe—and most importantly the French conquest—affected its history and ultimate destiny. Finally, I wanted to explore the origins of the American involvement in South Vietnam and to show how this involvement grew from a minor to a major factor in American affairs.

This is essentially a book about power, politics and people. I have told the story of Vietnam from its ancient beginnings and traced its course over two thousand years of its history. I think the reader will find this history interesting and useful, especially where it sheds light on today's events, many of which have deep roots in the past.

Much prominence in the earlier sections is given to the parts played by France and some Frenchmen in shaping the history of modern Vietnam. If there seems to be undue emphasis on this, to the neglect of the Vietnamese, it was only because it seemed to me more meaningful in terms of the story I wished to tell.

This book is not a history of Vietnam in the usual sense. It does not, except indirectly, discuss its geography or its economy, its culture or its customs, its different peoples or its religions. Such information can be found in excellent books already available.

Because I was writing a political history, I focused mainly on men and events. A short book on a big subject covering a long time span has its limitations. I had to be selective in my choice of material and leave out much that was important and relevant. There are, however, other works that deal more extensively with matters only touched upon in my book and the interested reader is advised to consult them if he wishes to find out more.

This book owes much to other books and authors, on whom I have had to rely for different areas of the Vietnam story. I have read a great deal about Vietnam and Asia: books, pamphlets, periodicals and newspapers. They were all helpful, but some were more useful than others, and I wish to acknowledge my debt to them.

The best—and only—history of Vietnam in English is Joseph Buttinger's *The Smaller Dragon*. This monumental survey of the Vietnamese past, which takes the story up to 1900, is indispensable for an understanding of the early period and the French conquest. My opening chapters lean heavily on Mr. Buttinger's admirable book.

The story of Vietnam under French rule can be found in Ellen Hammer's *The Struggle for Indochina*. Miss Hammer's book, which ends just before the close of the first Indochina war in 1954, is invaluable for its detailed treatment of Vietnam in modern times, particularly of the years since 1940.

Bernard Fall's thoughtful, fact-packed study, *The Two Viet-Nams*, gives a thorough picture of North Vietnam and South Vietnam in all their different aspects—governmental, political, economic and military. My biographical data about Ho Chi Minh and Ngo Dinh Diem are drawn largely from Fall, although I have supplemented these portraits with material from other sources. Mr. Fall's *Street of Joy*, a classic account of the two Indochina wars, is also recommended, as is a recent collection of his articles, *Viet-Nam Witness*.

Hoang Van Chi's *From Colonialism to Communism* is an insider's look at the political evolution of modern Vietnam, the rise of communism, and its triumph in the north. Mr. Chi writes from personal knowledge of the nationalist and communist movements in his country. It was my privilege earlier this year to meet and talk to this gentle, soft-spoken scholar in Washington, D.C., where he lives and works today. My account of the growth of nationalist groups in Vietnam is based on the description of such organizations in his book.

Before the United States took on its role in Vietnam, there were few books in English on the subject. Since then, the number of such books has grown and is still growing. They occupy, as of the present time, two shelves in my own library. In addition to the books already mentioned, there were many others I found valuable. Of these, I will cite only the following:

The Roots of French Imperialism in East Asia by John F. Cady; *Government and Politics of Southeast Asia,* edited by George McT. Kahin; *South Vietnam: Nation Under Stress* by Robert Scigliano; *U.S. Army Area Handbook for Vietnam* by Foreign Studies Division of The American University; *The New Face of War* by Malcolm W. Browne; *The Lost Revolution* by Robert Shaplen; *The Last Confucian* by Denis Warner; *The Making of a Quagmire* by David Halberstam; *Mission in Torment* by John Mecklin; *Vietnam: A Diplomatic Tragedy* by Victor Bator; *Communism in North Vietnam* by P. J. Honey; *North Vietnam Today,* edited by P. J. Honey; *The Viet-Nam Reader,* edited by Marcus G. Raskin and Bernard B. Fall; *Vietnam,* edited by Marvin E. Gettleman; *Conflict in the Shadows* by James E. Cross; *Modern Guerrilla Warfare,* edited by Franklin M. Osanka; *Communist Revolutionary Warfare* by George K. Tanham.

Needless to say, the interpretations of fact and the opinions that the reader will encounter in this book belong to the author alone.

Chapter 1

PEOPLE
OF THE
RED RIVER

WE begin with a question and a mystery. Who are the Vietnamese? We know, vaguely, that they descend from a non-Chinese, Mongoloid people who, in ancient times, left their tribal lands in south China and settled in the Red River country of what is now North Vietnam. Little else is clear. The origins of the Vietnamese, like those of all Southeast Asians, are obscure. Southeast Asia, a huge area lying between India and China, is a melting pot of peoples who have crossed and crisscrossed the continent for centuries. These migrations, in periodic waves and trickles, are still going on.

The early history of Vietnam is glorified by legend. Old tales tell of a Vietnamese kingdom in south China that existed three thousand years before the birth of Christ. Its name was said to be Van Lang, or Van Tang, which means "country of the tattooed men." These stories are part of folklore, but some people still believe them to be true.

Chinese annals, dating from the pre-Christian era, are the first writings to mention the Vietnamese. In them we are told of a kingdom named Nam-Viet in the south of China, which was founded by Trieu Da, a rebel Chinese general, in 208 B.C. Nam-Viet translates as "people of the

South." The members of the various tribes in that region came to be called Viets. Under Trieu Da, the Viets enlarged their domains by crossing the border southward into the northern part of today's Vietnam. The primitive people they found there they drove forcibly into the mountains. These tribesmen whom they met and defeated in the valleys of the Red River were of Malayo-Indonesian stock. Their descendants still inhabit the same mountains to which their forebears fled more than two thousand years ago. Little has changed about them. They are still primitive and illiterate; for them time has stood still.

The Viets found the new land to their liking. The soil was rich, and there was good hunting and fishing. In China, however, a warlike Han dynasty was beginning to press hard on Nam-Viet's south China preserves. The Viets were unable to resist this Chinese tide and were slowly pushed back into the sanctuary of the Red River country. There, for almost a hundred years, they fought off periodic incursions by the probing and relentless Han. In 111 B.C., they could hold out no longer. Nam-Viet fell to the Chinese, and its days of independence were over. For one thousand years thereafter, except for brief periods when they threw out the Chinese, the Vietnamese lived in bondage to their Chinese overlords. As a new province (for that is the way the Chinese thought of it), Nam-Viet was given a new name, Giao Chi, and a governor to run its affairs. The Han also installed military garrisons and kept enough troops on hand to maintain order and suppress rebellions.

Chinese occupation had a deep and long-lasting effect on Vietnam. Its people had been a simple farming, fishing and hunting folk when the Chinese first came. Although they had already learned to make and use iron and bronze, their lives were crude and their culture primitive. Most of their tools, implements and weapons were made of stone, such as the hoe, the knife, the spear and the axe. They had also become expert marksmen with the bow and arrow, which they used for hunting and for war.

Of farming the Viets knew little, except for some elementary methods of irrigation. On their farms, which had been laid out on land cleared by burning, they grew cereal grains mostly. But they knew nothing of the plow. They did not even know how to make use of the water buffalo

18

as a work animal. The Chinese showed them how to use both. The Chinese also taught them the difficult art of rice planting and cultivation. In this way did rice come to a land where it became the mainstay of life for its people.

The Chinese also brought engineering techniques to Vietnam. New roads and harbors were built, as were military fortifications and waterworks. From Chinese culture, the feudal Viets took much, including Chinese writing skills and learning. This brought a higher level of civilization to the Viets, but it was not enough to make the people content, nor to make them yearn any less for freedom.

At first, the Chinese were lenient in the way they ruled the Viets. Then, as the years passed, they began to interfere more and more in the affairs of the feudal lords and to gather greater power in their hands. There were several revolts, but these the Chinese put down with great severity. The first successful uprising by the Viets occurred in 39 A.D. It followed the execution by the government of a rebellious feudal lord, an act intended to frighten the other lords into submission. But the execution had the opposite effect. Instead of cowing the lords, it united them, and they mounted an army against the Chinese.

The rebels were led by two of the most remarkable women in Vietnamese history. One was Trung Trac, wife of the slain feudal lord; the other was her sister, Trung Nhi. After driving the Chinese from the country, the Trung sisters were proclaimed joint queens of the land. The new kingdom—or queendom—lasted only two years. In 42 A.D., the Chinese launched another invasion and defeated the armies of the Trung sisters. Their cause hopelessly lost, the sister queens took their own lives by leaping into a river and drowning. Today they are remembered in Vietnam in much the same way that Joan of Arc is remembered in France, and there are many statues in their honor.

The revolt taught the Chinese a lesson in how to run a conquered country. They stripped the Vietnamese feudal lords of all their governing powers. They sent more Chinese into the country and granted them even greater social and economic advantages. By the time they were through making changes, the Chinese had entirely revamped the power structure. No Vietnamese, for example, could work for the government in any capacity unless he agreed to be trained and educated in the Chinese way. And even then he was allowed to hold only minor posts.

The Chinese in Vietnam became a privileged elite. Among them there arose a class of great landowners whose Vietnamese wives bore them children of a new breed, neither wholly Chinese nor wholly Vietnamese. As the years passed, something strange began to happen to the members of this imported upper class. They began to look upon Vietnam as their own country and to think of the distant Chinese imperial power as an outside, alien force. Those with large estates wished to run their own local affairs without meddling by the central government. They also wanted taxes kept low. The government, of course, sought to keep them high. In short, the attitudes of the new elite became the same as those of the native Vietnamese feudal lords. This led to frequent clashes with the regime and finally to armed rebellion in 248 A.D.

The revolt was notable for two things. The first was that it failed. The second was that it gave Vietnamese history another heroic figure, again a woman. The name of this martial lady aristocrat was Thieu Au. Clad in golden armor and riding an elephant, she led an army of one thousand men into battle against the Chinese. But her army lost, and Thieu Au—perhaps remembering the Trung sisters—took her own life.

One more rebellion in 542 A.D. vanquished the Chinese for a short time, but all the others, in between, were failures. It would take a few more hundred years before the Vietnamese were to find the key to successful revolt.

That key, when it was found, was a simple one. It was to enlist the support of *all* the people. The armed struggles thus far had been mainly between local lords and the central government. Most of the people—which meant the peasants—rarely, if ever, took part in these conflicts. Thus, the rebel armies were always small in numbers and easily defeated.

Ly Bon, another national hero of Vietnam, is a good example of such a rebel leader. It was he who defeated and drove out the Chinese in 542. A rich landowner, Ly Bon was descended from Chinese who had come into Vietnam generations earlier. Grievances against the imperial power pushed him into open revolt. Success in the field won him a

20

kingdom, but he was not to wear the crown long. Two years later, he lost both crown and head when the Chinese returned to unseat him.

Such experiences would have disheartened most people, for Chinese power, as the centuries moved along, seemed to grow even greater and more invincible. But the Vietnamese would give up neither their pride nor their hope. Their goal was freedom—even if it took a thousand years.

In the eighth and ninth centuries came the first real sign that freedom might actually be won some day. Upper class revolutionaries, seeking mass support, began to agitate the peasant and to point out their common interest in a land freed from Chinese rule. Because they needed the peasant, the upper classes changed their attitude toward him. No longer did they treat him as an object of disdain, someone to be used and abused, like the water buffalo who helped him work the land. The Vietnamese peasant responded to this appeal. Soon a new kind of revolt was to flare up. For the first time, aristocrat and peasant would march together to meet the Chinese in battle. Crushed once, they rose again. And again. The key was found at last, but it would take time to build the alliance into a national force.

The alliance between peasant and master grew stronger. All the Vietnamese needed now was the historical moment —the right set of conditions—that would enable them to strike. That opportunity came in the early part of the tenth century when the ruling Tang dynasty began to weaken. The Tang had ruled in China for nearly three hundred years. Now their time of decline had come. The cause of their downfall was the same disease that had destroyed the Han, who had come before them as China's imperial family. It was, in brief, the exploitation of the Chinese peasant by wealthy landowners whose greed had no limits. Continuous peasant revolts, often led by bandit chieftains, shook the house of Tang and finally toppled it.

It was against this background of Chinese troubles that the Vietnamese launched a new, great uprising in 939. This time the Chinese were faced by a united people and an outstanding military leader, General Ngo Quyen. Their armies routed, the Chinese retreated across the border. Vietnam was free at last. After the death of Ngo Quyen, the dragon empire tried again in 946 to retake Vietnam but failed. For some twenty years thereafter local Viet-

21

namese leaders fought among themselves to see who would be ruler of the country. In 968, one of them, Dinh Bo Linh, won out over the others. He then had himself declared king and emperor.

Dinh Bo Linh was a shrewd ruler. More than anything else, Vietnam now needed peace. So the new emperor sought through diplomacy to placate the Chinese giant to the north. Emissaries were sent to the court of the Chinese emperor to work out a settlement between the two countries. The agreement they reached established nominal Chinese suzerainty over Vietnam, which meant, of course, that it was authority in name only. Dinh Bo Linh agreed to accept the title of vassal king and to pay tribute every three years to the Chinese emperor. The Chinese in turn agreed not to renew their attacks and to let the Vietnamese live in peace. Dinh Bo Linh was also permitted to use the title of emperor in his own country and in his relations with other states.

With their northern borders thus secure, the Vietnamese were ready to embark on conquests of their own. Their neighbor to the south was the kingdom of Champa which had been founded by seafaring Indian adventurers in the second century. The Chams had vast stretches of fertile lands that the Vietnamese had been eyeing hungrily for some time. A maritime people who lived by fishing and by trade, the Chams had slowly let their agriculture fall into neglect. A slow trickle of Viet farmers began to move into the rich plains of the Cham empire and to farm the land.

At first, the Chams did not object, for the land was not being used, anyway. But when more Vietnamese came and their settlements began to grow, the Chams put up opposition. Clashes followed, which led to war between the two kingdoms. Warfare between Viets and Chams lasted many years, and the fortunes of war seesawed back and forth between them. But the Vietnamese always gained from these conflicts, each time adding more slices of Cham territory to their growing domains. No state could long endure this continual process of erosion. By 1471, the once-great Cham empire was reduced to mere slivers of land. A century and a half later it had vanished altogether, leaving behind some crumbling watchtower ruins to mark its passing. Today, Vietnam has a small number of Chams living in the south, the dwindling remnants of a mighty past.

This policy of land-grabbing had worked so well against the Chams that the Vietnamese continued it against the Khmer empire in Cambodia. Ex-soldiers of the Vietnamese army were given tracts of free land on distant frontiers of the south country. There they set up settlements and communities, worked hard, and prospered. Hardened combat veterans, they were a tough breed, ready to defend their new lands and eager to acquire more. Across the border, in neighboring Cambodia, were lush, inviting deltas. The Vietnamese farmer-soldier marched in, staked out a piece of land and dared anyone to take it away from him. Border skirmishes flamed into bitter warfare. Like the hapless Chams, the Khmers, too, fell before the Viets. So complete was their defeat that in the year 1660 they started paying a regular tribute to their imperialist neighbor.

The most astonishing fact about the expansionist drive of the Vietnamese is that it took place while they were fighting a civil war among themselves. This conflict between rival feudal families in the north and the south raged for two hundred years, from the sixteenth to the eighteenth centuries, with occasional periods of truce. The north was dominated by the great house of Trinh, which controlled the emperors of the reigning Le dynasty. The rule of the Trinh was contested by the Nguyen clan, which ran the southern provinces as its private domain.

Though the Trinh had the more powerful armies, they were still unable to defeat the Nguyen, on whose territories the battles were mainly fought. The difficult terrain, with its jungles, mountains and swamps, gave the defenders a military advantage. But there was another reason why the stronger Trinh could not overcome the Nguyen. The latter had greater support among their people. The peasants in the south were more prosperous than those in the north where land had become scarce. During the wars between Trinh and Nguyen, many northern peasants left their homes and moved to the south where there was free land and greater opportunity.

As barriers against invasion, the Nguyen built two huge protective walls which stood only a few miles from the line that now divides North from South Vietnam at the

17th parallel. This fact, of no great significance in itself, is another reminder, however, that the division of Vietnam into two halves is not a new experience for its people. Northerners and southerners, from the start, felt themselves to be different. The north, as the older part of the country, thought itself more truly Vietnamese, while the south, a restless, moving, growing frontier region, was rawer, richer and freer. These differences of outlook and temperament persist to this very day.

We have seen that the long civil war did not stop the country from growing. Neither did it upset the well-ordered patterns of daily life, which were the same as they had been for centuries. Society had long since settled down into a mold of law and custom that had everyone fixed in his proper and rightful place. The Vietnamese were guided in these arrangements by the great philosopher Confucius, whose doctrines had been taught them by the Chinese. The emperor, as head of the state, stood at the top of the social pyramid. Below him came nobles, officials, priests, scholars, landowners, soldiers, merchants and artisans. At the very bottom of the pyramid, holding the whole structure up, so to speak, was the great peasant mass. All, however, were part of the nation-family for whom the emperor was both father figure and supreme religious leader. It was the common belief that in this latter role the emperor could communicate directly with the very powers of heaven.

The administration of the state was run by a civil service whose officials, called mandarins, were ranked in nine separate grades. To become a mandarin, one had to compete in public examinations which were open to all. Though a peasant, in theory, could become a mandarin, in practice, he rarely did. An applicant had to know the Chinese classics and excel at literary composition; and only the rich had time for such pursuits.

It was this kind of world, solidly rooted in tradition and the past, that the first Europeans encountered when they came to Vietnam in the sixteenth century.

In 1498, the great Portuguese explorer Vasco da Gama arrived in India, the first European to make his way to the Asian continent by sea. This meeting of East and West was to have crucial consequences for the future. It opened the way for fleets of foreign ships that came with goods to sell and left with their holds bulging with Asian wares and spices. At first, only the Portuguese benefited from this rich trade; later the rest of Europe would follow her lead.

This was the period when Portugal and Spain were the great sea powers of Europe, and no other European state dared to challenge their supremacy. While the Portuguese were making their inroads in Asia, the Spanish were doing the same in another area of the Pacific world: the Philippines. The first Portuguese trading post was set up in the Indian enclave of Goa. More followed quickly, until they stretched across land and sea in a sweeping arc from India to Japan.

A Portuguese sea captain named Antonia de Faria was the first European to sail a ship into Vietnamese waters in 1535. Like his compatriots elsewhere, he had come to trade. Soon another trading post was added to the growing list flying the Portuguese flag. The name Cochinchina was first applied to Vietnam by these early sea adventurers who thought that its Chinese name of Giao Chi (which they pronounced "Kutchi") sounded too much like Cochin, one of their colonies in India. To distinguish the two from each other, Vietnam, because it was close to China, was called Cochinchina.

For a hundred years the Portuguese had Vietnamese trade all to themselves. Then, in 1636, the Dutch arrived and gave them competition. By then the power of Portugal and Spain was being eclipsed. The defeat of the Spanish Armada by the English in 1588 had dealt a crippling blow to the Hispanic empires. As England and Holland grew stronger, Spain and Portugal grew weaker. The seventeenth and eighteenth centuries would witness the triumph of the English and Dutch in Asia, and the complete decline of their two rivals.

When the Dutch came to Vietnam they cut into the century-old Portuguese monopoly. There was lots of money to be made in the arms business, for the civil war between Trinh and Nguyen was then at its height. The Dutch built factories in the north and sold weapons to the Trinh, while the Portuguese supplied the Nguyen with their military equipment. It was a profitable enterprise while it lasted, but when the warring Vietnamese patched up their differences in a temporary truce, trade began to fall off. Its decline after that was precipitous, and by the end of the century it had virtually reached bottom. So both competitors did the only sensible thing under the circumstances. They left. The only Europeans who stayed were a few merchants and a growing number of Catholic missionaries.

The early missionaries had come to Vietnam hard on the heels of the first Portuguese traders. Catholicism, then the great reigning religion in Europe, considered it a duty to carry the word of God to heathen lands. Asia was fresh territory for its missionary work and Portugal became the principal agent of this eastward movement by the Church. In return, the Portuguese were allowed to control the selection of missionaries sent to Asia. Any priest embarking for the Orient had to board ship in Lisbon. From there he sailed to Portugal's colony of Goa in India, where he underwent close scrutiny by the colonial authorities. If approved, he traveled on to his destination. If, however, he was found unacceptable, he was unceremoniously shipped back to Europe.

Little is known about these early missionaries to Vietnam. Many did important work; but of those we know about, only two were really outstanding. Both of these eminent churchmen were French; both were remarkable; and both won lasting places in Vietnamese history.

Monsignor Alexander of Rhodes was the first of this notable pair. He was thirty-four, already in mid-career, when he was assigned to do missionary work in Vietnam. From the moment of his arrival there in 1626, the fortunes of the Church took an upward turn. For years, Church scholars had been trying to adapt the Vietnamese language to our own Latin alphabet. This immensely difficult project had made some headway, but it still was unfinished when Rhodes arrived. His completion of the alphabet, which made possible a new system of writing called Quoc Ngu, was a monumental feat of scholarship. Europeans could now read Vietnamese for the first time. They were also able to translate their own books into Quoc Ngu so that they could be read by the Vietnamese. This revolutionary breakthrough in communication, of which Rhodes was the prime mover, brought the two civilizations face to face in a new and more meaningful way.

In 1627 Rhodes traveled to Hanoi where he made a great impression on all he met, both royalty and plain people. His intelligence was keen, his convictions strong, and his powers of persuasion great. In two years, by his own count, he made 6,700 converts. Most of them came from the ranks of the poor, but some of the new Catholics he brought into the Church were rich, and some were even of royal blood. Rhodes was, as a matter of fact, too persuasive, for in 1630 he was told to leave the country. The Vietnamese rulers were beginning to understand that in Christianity they faced a different kind of challenge and danger, one that would threaten their age-old institutions if it was allowed to grow and spread. The exile of Rhodes from Vietnam is proof that he had done his work well. This is all the more impressive when we consider his brief stay there of only five years.

From his new vantage point in the Portuguese colony of Macao, in south China, Rhodes continued to keep an eye on Vietnamese affairs. He kept urging the Church in Rome to make needed reforms in the land he had learned to love. The right to control the selection of priests, he believed, should be taken away from the Portuguese and returned to the Church where it properly belonged. He also proposed that a number of priests should be recruited from among the Vietnamese themselves, for only then would Catholicism become firmly rooted among the people. Rhodes lived long enough to see his suggestions adopted in 1658. Two years later, on a new assignment to Persia, he died, leaving behind a legacy of good works and great deeds.

We must jump a century ahead now to focus on the life and career of our second great cleric, Pigneau de Behaine. This extraordinary French priest was only twenty-six years old when he reached Vietnam, or Cochinchina, the name by which he knew it, in 1767. Three years later, at the age of twenty-nine, he was made a bishop. But the young bishop, who had had his fair share of adventure already in this strange country, was fated for still more. A dramatic, unexpected turn of events would literally change his life and reshape his destiny.

In 1772, Vietnam was set aflame again by rebellion. This revolt was different from any that had come before, for it was based on an alliance between the peasantry and the new, emerging class of small merchants. Combining their forces, the two groups had a single aim: to overthrow the old order. The rebels were led by three brothers with the same family name as the lords of the south—Nguyen. They were not, however, related. The revolt, called the Tay Son rebellion, took its name from the village where it started, and the brothers, too, came to be known as the Tay Son.

When the uprising began, Vietnam was still ruled by Trinh and Nguyen in their separate realms of north and south. The rebellion of the Tay Son struck first at the Nguyen in the south. Their armies, growing in number as they went, swept all before them. By 1777, every last member of the Nguyen clan, except one, was destroyed. The one exception was the sixteen-year-old Prince Nguyen Anh, who in that same year fled the avenging Tay Son and found sanctuary with the Catholic Bishop Pigneau de Behaine. Pigneau took the young prince in and gave him shelter. From the very moment he performed this act of mercy, the life of the youthful prelate changed and took on new meaning. To take sides in a revolt is a political act, and Pigneau understood this very well. He had made his choice; now he would have to stand or fall by it. There was a personal side as well to Pigneau de Behaine's decision, for the bishop, a man of large ambition, had plans of his own for conquest and empire. The remaining twenty years of his life would be spent in pursuit of two main goals—to make his young prince an emperor and to win Cochinchina for France.

This must have seemed, at the time, like a mad dream, for the Tay Son, with their powerful armies, had until then been unbeatable. Soon afterward, they would begin their march to the north which was to end in 1786 in the total defeat of the Trinh. A year after that, when the last Le emperor fled from the country, Vietnam would at last be reunified under the dictatorship of the Tay Son.

All these events still lay ahead, in the year 1778, when Prince Nguyen Anh came out of hiding and returned to the wars. The army he gathered was a mixture of loyal old followers, hired mercenaries and Chinese pirates, and with Pigneau at his side he forged it into an efficient fighting force. As the Tay Son moved northward, the teen-age prince retook several provinces and the key port of Saigon. There, for four years, he ruled as king of Cochinchina. His mentor, guide and overall strategist during this period was the good Bishop Pigneau who did not feel at all strange in this new role of soldier-diplomat.

Then, in 1782, the Tay Son returned and shattered the prince's armies with an unexpected lightning attack by sea. In Thailand, where they took refuge, Nguyen Anh and Bishop Pigneau considered their next move. Pigneau advised that help be sought from a foreign power, which in his scheme of things could only mean France. When Nguyen Anh agreed, Pigneau set out on a journey that occupies a special place in the annals of diplomacy and warfare. He went first to Pondicherry, last remnant of the shrinking French empire in India. There, after months of talks and negotiations, Pigneau failed to convince Governor Conway and the French military that they should lend the distant Vietnamese prince their support. Pigneau then made the long voyage back to France where, in a brilliant diplomatic campaign, he won the hardheaded ministers of Louis XVI to his side.

When the triumphant bishop returned to Pondicherry in 1788, he now came as his majesty's "Royal Commissioner for Cochinchina" who had in his possession a treaty of alliance between the king of France and the king of Cochinchina. The terms of the treaty called for the French to supply Nguyen Anh with military assistance, in return for which France was to be given certain territories outright, plus exclusive trading rights and privileges. Pigneau now called on Governor Conway to live up to France's side of the bargain. What Pigneau did not know was that Conway had received secret instructions from the French foreign minister, who had obviously had second thoughts about the deal he had made with Nguyen Anh's representative. The instructions granted the Governor the power to decide whether or not to give Pigneau the soldiers and arms he needed. To the bishop's dismay, Conway, who really opposed French expansion in Asia, said no to his request. Pigneau was stunned. The game, it seemed, had ended for him in complete failure, but this indomitable man would still not give up. In a letter written at this time, he stated defiantly, "I shall make the revolution in Cochinchina alone." And that is just about what he did.

Turned down by Conway, Pigneau now began filling the

ears of local French merchants with his schemes and pleas. Slowly, he won pledges of support and the money needed to mount a campaign against the Tay Son. A trip to the nearby Mascarene Islands brought in more funds. In June, 1789, the fighting bishop set sail for Vietnam. His fleet of two ships carried men, guns and ammunition, all paid for with the money he had wheedled out of the French merchants. One month later, in far off France, the storming of the Bastille would light up the sky with the first lightning flash of the coming French Revolution.

The revolution in France, when it came, put an end to all thoughts about empire in Asia. The treaty with Cochinchina became a curiosity piece that had been rendered obsolete by history. To Prince Nguyen Anh, this was just as well, for he really didn't relish turning over part of his country to the French. For Pigneau de Behaine, however, it was the end of a dream. All that remained of it was the desire to see Nguyen Anh installed as emperor of Cochinchina. But even that moment was denied him. During the next ten years, an endless series of campaigns against the Tay Son brought victory nearer and nearer. Much credit belonged to Pigneau, for it was due mainly to the superiority of French arms that Nguyen Anh was winning. But when Pigneau de Behaine died in 1799, final victory was still three years away. The prince had his good friend and companion-in-arms buried with all the honors due a royal duke. Pigneau's accomplishments had indeed been noteworthy, but he had failed at the two things he wanted most to achieve—to carve out an empire for France and to convert Nguyen Anh to Christianity so that Cochinchina would be ruled by its first Catholic emperor.

It is therefore ironic to note that under the dynasty founded by Nguyen Anh when he did become emperor, Catholics were more violently persecuted than they had ever been before. This dynasty was founded in 1802 after the fall of the Tay Son. Prince Nguyen Anh became the Emperor Gia Long, and it was as Gia Long that he restored to the country its ancient name of Vietnam. During his lifetime, he still maintained friendly relations with the French and tolerated the Christian religion. But his successor, Minh Mang, who ruled from 1820 and 1841, changed this policy. As the European powers became more aggressive in Asia, so, too, did Asian feeling against the West

30

grow more bitter. In Vietnam this hostility, mixed with fear, gave rise to a government-sponsored campaign against Catholics, which was to bring the emperors into direct conflict with France.

Chapter 2

THREAT FROM THE WEST

THE destiny of Vietnam, although its people were unaware of it then, was being decided by a new kind of revolution that had been building up in Europe for a hundred years or more and would really burst forth during the nineteenth century. This new upheaval was the Industrial Revolution. It had nothing to do with politics or the overthrowing of governments. It was an economic revolution of men and machines that had already worked enormous changes in the lives of people and the affairs of nations. Under its impact, European feudalism, with its lords and serfs, its fiefs and manors, was being replaced by a new system—capitalism—whose mainstays were businessmen, bankers, merchants, workers, and inventors. Like all great historical movements, industrialism developed slowly, so that its first accomplishments, dramatic though they were, hardly prepared anyone for what lay ahead. Yet the signs pointing to the future were all there, for those who cared to look.

A man named James Watt, for instance, had trapped a powerful source of non-human energy inside a steam engine and put it to work. Marvelous new machinery was being invented that made it possible for men to produce and sell more goods than they ever had before. Towns that had become cities were growing and spreading. Farmers pushed off their farms were turning into city workers who made their livings in workshops called factories. All this energy and drive, which was transforming the face of Europe, would soon be making itself felt in other parts of the world. Asia and Africa would feel its effects, and so, too, would a struggling new republic in North America, the United States.

Even wars helped speed up the process, for they always brought great technical progress. In the latter part of the eighteenth century and the early part of the nineteenth, there was a series of European wars that lasted almost twenty-five years. First it was revolutionary France that put the continent to the torch. For ten years, from 1792 to 1802, its armies were almost constantly on the march. No sooner had that menace ceased than another took its place—Napoleon. This Corsican upstart, who rose from general to emperor, proved an even greater threat. For thirteen years, Napoleon kept the whole of Europe in a state of panic and alert. As a result, its statesmen had little time for anything but the affairs of Europe. Only after Napoleon had been stopped and put away for good on the island of St. Helena did Europe breathe freely again and turn to other matters.

As the continent settled down to normal, business and trade picked up and faraway places like Asia took on added importance. The Asian trade had been lagging, but now there were good reasons for reviving it. Men were discovering to their amazement that an industrial society, even in its infant stages, has appetites and capacities that get bigger every year. Asia as a market and as a source of raw materials began to look more and more attractive. England, the leading industrial and sea power, was in the forefront of this new turn to the East. Before long the nation known as the shopkeeper of the world would also be the owner of the world's greatest empire. To own colonies was not only a mark of prestige; it was also sound business.

Vietnam, just like other Asian countries, found itself caught up in the new wave of European interest. This fresh surge of attention worried its rulers. There had been no such threat during most of Gia Long's reign when Europe had been bogged down in its long struggle with Napoleon. The century had started out well for the Vietnamese. The war with the Tay Son, which had dragged on for thirty years, was over. There was, for the first time in several centuries, genuine unity in the country. China no longer represented a danger, nor did other neighboring states. As for the French, they were certainly no menace at this time. Some Frenchmen still dreamed of empire in Vietnam, but they were few indeed. Pigneau de Behaine had stirred many imaginations with his visions of imperial glory in Asia, and the force of his arguments had left lingering traces in certain quarters. Half a century later, these ideas would come to life again, but in the days of Napoleon nobody really took them seriously.

Even after the fall of Napoleon, French aims in Vietnam were modest. Their first probing efforts, made in 1817, were offers of trade and diplomatic relations. Gia Long, who was opposed to trade with the West, turned them down. He had similarly rejected the English when they wished to trade with him earlier in the century. The emperor refused all business dealings with Europeans because he feared the effects of foreign contact. Only under conditions of war and military necessity had he purchased goods from Europe, but as soon as that need had ceased the trade had ceased as well. Vietnam had been lucky in avoiding foreign alliances and entanglements. The closest it had come to anything like that had been the Treaty of 1787 which Pigneau de Behaine had signed with the regime of prerevolutionary France. Fortunately for Gia Long, however, the treaty had never gone into effect, so that its provisions remained a dead letter. Pigneau had wanted that treaty with all his heart, but he had then worked just as hard to get support for his royal friend from other sources. Better still, from the Vietnamese point of view, they had not been forced to give up either territory or special privileges in return for this help.

Gia Long was still paying back the money he had borrowed for his campaign against the Tay Son. But these were private debts that did not obligate him in any way to outside governments. Trade with the West, he felt, would eventually lead to such obligations and give Europe more of a say in the affairs of his country. It would also open the door even more to those pernicious Occidental ideas that had already disrupted Vietnamese society and corrupted some of its people. To Gia Long and his mandarins, this was the most important factor in their decision not to trade. Further contamination could be prevented by a firm policy of isolation and exclusion. By sealing off their borders, they would keep out the foreigner and his alien ways.

Unfortunately, there were already foreigners in Vietnam —the missionaries. As long as they remained in the country, it would not be free of European influence. To the Vietnamese ruling class, few of whom were Christians, the missionaries were a subversive lot, a fifth column that sought political as well as spiritual power. A missionary might call himself a servant of God, but a Frenchman, after all, was still a Frenchman, even in clerical garb. Where did his loyalty really lie—to his God or to his native land? The Vietnamese rulers drew the blanket conclusion that no missionary could be trusted. It would be wiser and safer to ban their doctrines and drive them from the land. While Gia Long sat on the throne, however, the memory of Pigneau de Behaine stayed his hand, and Catholics were not molested. The emperors who followed him to the throne were not bound by this moral obligation.

Under Minh Mang, Thieu Tri and Tu Duc—the last three monarchs of a free Vietnam—the attitudes toward Europe and the missionaries hardened. Minh Mang was the first to take official action against the Catholics. His first decrees were relatively mild. They prohibited missionaries from entering the country and also placed restrictions on the preaching and spreading of the Christian doctrine. Gradually, however, the laws grew more severe, and these same activities became crimes punishable by death. In 1833, the first missionary was executed. When several others met similar fates, the French protested the executions, which had been carried out in a most brutal manner. In France they were greeted with horror, but the government could do nothing to avenge them unless it wished to go to war. It didn't—at least, not yet. In the meantime, the emperors, who were determined to wipe out the disease of westernism, continued to strike at its roots through the Church.

The policy of isolation, begun under Gia Long, became even more narrow and suspicious. It was firmly supported by the ruling mandarin elite who believed that only by putting a wall between themselves and the outside world could they save their country and the social system on

35

which their power rested. Only two states—Japan and Thailand—withstood the new march of Europe through Asia, and both escaped only because they adapted to the challenge by changing their old ways and institutions. The rulers of Vietnam did not. Therein lies the major reason for their downfall and ultimate conquest by the French.

Still, Vietnam did not lose its independence at a single stroke. Its demise came slowly, in stages. The country was gobbled up a piece at a time by the French who waited until mid-century before they struck. Until this belated drive for empire began, French policy in Asia had been uncertain about its goals. Its real target was China, already under severe attack by competing European states. French mercantile interests in Asia wanted a base of operations from which they could launch their assault on the rich Chinese market. There, as everywhere else, they had to contend with the English. It was getting to be an old story. First they had fought them for the North American continent and lost. This was followed by their duel for India, where France had also been bested. Now here they both were again, jockeying for position in Asia. The French were getting a little tired of playing second fiddle to the British. Their national pride needed a boost, but they were not ready yet to make a major move in the East.

French efforts thus far had been less than spectacular. While their leaders hesitated, other European nations were making great strides in Asia. French admirals fumed because there were English and Dutch ports in the Far East where French ships could put in, but not one port that flew the French flag. This, from their point of view, was intolerable and degrading. The navy, which had a responsibility to protect France's interests abroad, became the loudest champion of empire in Asia. It found allies among the missionaries who wished to see the spread of European power in the Orient. This was especially true in Vietnam where Catholics had suffered much for their faith. As the forces of European imperialism in Asia began to move into high gear, the alliance of the admirals and the Church grew stronger and more influential.

The British had shown the rest of Europe the way in China. That ancient empire had fallen on sad days. When it tested its armies against those of the West, it discovered to its astonishment that it was weak and vulnerable. Humbled in battle, the Chinese had to sign humiliating treaties forcing them to yield territory as well as other rights and privileges. The death knell for imperial China sounded in the Opium War of 1839. Opium had been brought into the country by the British, who found dealing in it a most profitable business. As the opium flowed in, Chinese silver flowed out into the pockets of British traders and investors. When the Chinese tried to stop this trade, the British went to war. For three years the conflict raged, and when it was over the beaten Chinese had to give up five key ports and the island of Hong Kong, which the British annexed outright. But that was only the beginning. Other countries followed Britain's lead, and China was gradually sliced up as neatly as a pie. France was among those who joined the robbers' feast.

After the British opened up China, Vietnam began to take on increasing importance in the French scheme of things. Admiral Cécille, commander of the Asian fleet, wanted bases from which his ships could operate. Some of the Vietnamese ports would have made ideal bases, but Premier François Guizot was afraid that if France took them over there would be conflict with England. So the French went elsewhere. They seized the island of Basilan in the Pacific, hoping to make it into the same kind of naval fortress that the English had in Hong Kong. But Spain protested, claiming that Basilan lay too close to the Philippines and was therefore within the Spanish sphere of interest. Clashes between French and Spanish ships resulted in a French withdrawal from the island.

France had another brush with a European power over Tahiti. When a French naval officer landed on the island and then laid claim to it as a protectorate, the English were incensed. Premier Guizot reacted fearfully as the British lion roared in anger. For awhile it looked as if there might be war. But the ruffled feelings of the English were finally soothed by a French offer to pay for the island. War was averted and France finally had a base in the Pacific. The government took both these incidents as a lesson, but the navy, still smarting under the setbacks, was ready to go on. As the next move on the Asian chessboard, it suggested Vietnam, but the wary Guizot vetoed the idea.

This spurt of European activity alarmed the Vietnamese. The meaning of the Opium War had not been lost on Emperor Minh Mang. While it was still in progress, he had sent envoys to Paris to conduct talks with the French. Even so rigid a man as the emperor had been shocked into taking action by the realization that a Chinese defeat would place his own country in jeopardy. He wanted to head off that danger by coming to an agreement with France and England. Perhaps if they heard the Vietnamese side of the case, they would understand that what lay behind his anti-missionary crusade was not cruelty but fear of the European. To show his good faith, Minh Mang was even willing to enter into commercial relations. This should have been bait for the French who had long been angling for trading privileges. But the government of King Louis Philippe did not trust Minh Mang. There was also opposition to negotiations from prominent Catholics who remained unforgiving. In this atmosphere, negotiation was impossible. The talks were broken off.

Rebuffed by the French, the envoys went to London where they had hopes of doing better. There, too, they met with disappointment. Protestant England had no religious argument to pick with the Vietnamese, but neither was it in the mood for talking.

In 1841, when the envoys returned to their native land, empty-handed, they learned that the Emperor Minh Mang had died in their absence. A new monarch, Thieu Tri, now ruled Vietnam. The failure of Minh Mang's mission convinced the new ruler that it would be pointless to try further diplomacy. The mood of isolation deepened. Persecution of Catholics, though sporadic, continued. France kept complaining but its complaints fell on deaf ears. Both Thieu Tri and his son, Tu Duc, who came after him, refused to drop their anti-Catholic campaigns. Some Vietnamese warned that it was dangerous to provoke the French, and that one day it would cause great trouble. But the men in power did not follow this counsel.

Still, the danger point had not been reached. Even as late as the 1840s, as we have seen, the French government was still uncommitted to a policy of conquest in Vietnam. Despite its irritation over the missionary question, France proceeded with caution and kept its official temper under control. There were occasional incidents of reprisal by the French navy, but these were mainly carried out by hot-headed officers who acted on their own. Such clashes had increased the bad feeling between both countries, but as long as Guizot, a political opponent of the Church, was premier there was little chance that France would go to war because of the Catholic issue. Only a change in government that would shift the political balance of power could lead to new policies and new decisions. The Revolution of 1848, which brought about the fall of Guizot, also set the stage for the coup d'etat of Louis-Napoleon in 1851.

This seizure of power in France by the nephew of the first Napoleon put the country in the hands of an adventurer who was to fight six major wars before he was undone by the Franco-Prussian War of 1870. Louis-Napoleon, later known as the Emperor Napoleon III, had strong backing in Catholic circles. Long unhappy about the persecution of their co-religionists in Vietnam, French Catholics were strong for intervention. Napoleon was not averse to their promptings, but there were delays. First he had to strengthen his government and his personal dictatorship. His fence-mending and political maneuvering occupied him for several years. Then, in 1853, the Crimean War broke out and France—along with England, Turkey and Sardinia—fought the Russians for three years. In 1857, however, Napoleon was ready to take the offensive in Asia. The pleas for intervention, from missionaries in Vietnam and from Catholics at home, had grown louder and more demanding. The new Bonaparte could no longer ignore them.

There were other compelling reasons, mainly economic, which also influenced Louis-Napoleon's decision to act. France's economy was unable to absorb the overflow of goods coming from its factories. The English and the Dutch had empires in Asia, which siphoned off their economic surpluses. French businessmen and economic planners began to clamor for similar Asian possessions. When a Special Commission on Cochinchina produced its report in 1857, which spoke of "the force of circumstances" that "pushes nations towards the Far East," it was clear that the time for action had come. In its conclusion, the Commission also put the following question to the government: "Are we going to be the only ones without possessions in the East, where the English, the Dutch, the Spanish, and even the Russians are building up their positions?" To this blunt query and challenge, the answer of Louis-Napoleon could only be a firm "No!"

The navy was given secret orders to attack. The government was also ready with an official excuse for the assault —the cruel and continued persecution of French and Spanish missionaries. To make the cover story more plausible, several Spanish ships joined the fleet under the command of French Admiral Rigault de Genouilly. On August 31, this Franco-Spanish squadron sailed into the Bay of Tourane and came in sight of the Vietnamese city bearing that name. On September 1, the city was shelled and then stormed by a landing party. The following day it fell to the invaders. The French had gained their first foothold in the country, and the drive for empire was under way.

Chapter 3

THE MARCH
OF CONQUEST

COCHINCHINA, as the French still called it, turned out to be harder to subdue than they had expected. If they had come looking for quick empire they were soon disappointed. Planted stories in the newspapers back home had prepared the French people for the attack on Tourane. These spoke of barbaric religious persecution no longer to be tolerated. They also pointed out that French ambitions in the Far East required a main strategic naval base. Tourane was to be that base from which the French would go on to even greater glory.

The hopes for rapid victory soon faded as terrain, weather and disease began to take their toll. The campaign itself had gotten off to a lurching start by a serious dispute inside the French camp. Bishop Pellerin, an important Catholic prelate who had sailed with the admiral as a guest aboard his flagship, *Nemesis,* had his own opinions about the best course of action to be taken. He argued that since most Christians were in Tonking, the northern part of the country, the French should now move in that direction. The admiral disagreed. From a military point of view, he felt that this would be a grave error. So Monsignor Pellerin was overruled. Instead of going north, the French forces veered south. Their target was the port of Saigon.

Admiral Genouilly picked Saigon for two reasons. It was the key to control of the rice bowl of the south. By capturing it he would cut off the supply of rice to the Vietnamese army and disrupt the economy of the north which depended on this rice. He was also convinced that one day Saigon would become a major port and an important center of world commerce. The French had no great difficulty in taking Saigon, which fell on February 17, 1859.

Then the admiral's troubles began. Attacks by the Emperor Tu Duc's troops kept him busy defending the areas he already held. Incessant rains made the treacherous terrain virtually impassable. There was also serious news from Tourane. The small force that had been left there to guard the city was under siege and in desperate straits. Genouilly had to cut short any plans he had for further action and go to the rescue.

Saigon remained in the hands of a strong French garrison while the admiral sailed north again to lift the siege at Tourane. There he found the French suffering more from sickness than from war. Cholera and typhus were killing twenty soldiers for every one killed in battle. Worse still, there would be no reinforcements coming from France. The admiral's request for more men had been turned down by Napoleon who had a new war on his hands with Austria. There was only one thing the tired and discouraged Genouilly could do. He asked Paris to replace him with another commander. The man who succeeded him, Admiral Page, took in the situation at a glance. Tourane —by now a disease-ridden graveyard—was abandoned. Saigon, already bustling with the coming and going of European ships, was told to hold out as best it could. Then Admiral Page sailed off to join a new Anglo-French expedition being mounted against China.

The eight hundred Frenchmen defending Saigon had to wait until 1861 before they got more help. Not until then did the wavering politicians in Paris decide to revive the stalled campaign in Vietnam. The architect of this fresh effort was Chasseloup-Laubat, a firm believer in empire who had just been appointed minister of marine and colonies. Seventy ships and 3,500 men spearheaded the new drive. When more men and ships were needed, France was quick to furnish them. In a little more than a year's time, on June 6, 1862, Tu Duc was compelled to sign a treaty that ceded the French their first big chunk of Vietnamese territory. They were given three provinces next to Saigon and the island of Poulo Condore which later became the site of a notorious French prison. In addition, France received other important concessions. European ships could now use three principal ports as entry points and engage in trade. French warships were given the right to sail freely up the Mekong River as far as Cambodia. There were to be no more restrictions placed on missionaries who could now preach as they pleased. No other European power was to be given even an inch of territory in Vietnam unless the French agreed to it. And for being so troublesome, Tu Duc had to pay France war damages of 4 million piastres.

The French did not wrest these gains from Tu Duc by military force alone. The emperor of Vietnam came to the treaty table because it seemed to him that he had no other choice. Materially, he had been weakened by the loss of rice from the south. This limited his ability to raise large armies simply because he was unable to feed them. His troops also lacked modern weapons and were thus no match for the French. These weapons could have been bought, but Tu Duc and his mandarins scorned their use. This may appear astonishing except when we remember the stubborn backwardness with which they approached all new problems and situations. They were in a fight to the death, but they would survive—or die—in their own way.

Another weakness that hampered the emperor in his war with the French was also of his own making. He just could not rouse his people to fight against the invader. In ancient times it had been the whole people that had risen as one to throw out the Chinese. But the people did not rally to the regime now. The peasant disliked the French, but he also hated the mandarin. In this hour of his country's gravest crisis, he avoided taking sides. While Tu Duc's armies grappled with the French, northern peasants launched a series of bitter rebellions. Then came another, even greater threat that almost toppled Tu Duc from his throne. This was a revolt in the north led by a pretender of the old Le dynasty, whose cause was supported by the missionaries and their Christian peasant followers. Tu Duc was too weak to wage war on several fronts. He chose to make temporary peace with the French and to fight his own people. First he had to save his own regime. There would be time enough later for settling scores with the French.

Admiral Bonard, the new French commander, had driven a hard bargain. It hurt the emperor's pride to sign the harsh treaty provisions, but he consoled himself with the thought that he had won a valuable delay and that time was on his side. Time would defeat the Europeans—time and the country itself. Even now French soldiers were suffering untold hardships from the climate and sickness. When their ranks had been thinned out enough by death and disease, they would get aboard their ships and go home. Then all would be well again, and the country could return to the way it had been before the foreigner had come.

It did not happen as Tu Duc had hoped. Instead of leaving, the French stayed. Instead of weakening, they grew stronger. Instead of being satisfied with what they had been given, they wanted more. In later years, Tu Duc must have pondered more than once the wisdom of his decision to turn over half the south to the French. It had established them firmly in the country as a sovereign power over a huge area. It had also exposed the weakness of the emperor and the fragile hold he had on his people. The respite he had gained from his truce with France enabled Tu Duc to crush the rebels in the north; but it did not put an end to French ambitions in Vietnam, which were tirelessly promoted by empire-minded politicians and adventurers.

In 1863, Admiral de la Grandière, the newly appointed governor of French Cochinchina, arrived to take up his duties. This aggressive, domineering man soon showed why he had been picked for the job. By the end of the year he had forced the weak king of Cambodia to sign a document that made his country a French protectorate. His appetite hardly whetted by this easily won prize, de la Grandière now began to eye the remaining three provinces that were still under Vietnamese rule. Not until the summer of 1867 was he ready to strike. When he did, there was little resistance. The campaign lasted barely a week. At its end, he proudly informed his government that it

44

now controlled all of the south. More than eight years had gone by since the French first landed at Tourane. How much longer would it take before they were masters of the entire country?

For a while, at least, they were content with what they had. There were enough problems in their new, enlarged colony of Cochinchina to keep them busy for some time. Officials had to be trained and brought in from France to run the government and the administration. The economy had to be made over so that it would begin to repay the huge investment that had so far been squandered on empire-building with little or no return. The growing hostility of the Vietnamese was also a vexing problem. Ever since Tu Duc had made them a present of their first three provinces, the French had been beset by a rash of local rebellions. The peasant, at first neutral in the struggle, had made the discovery that the new rulers were just as bad as his own mandarins when it came to exploitation. Peasant guerrilla bands kept lighting little fires of revolt all over the colony. As soon as the government put one out, another would flare up somewhere else. For the first time, the French knew what it was like to face organized resistance by sections of the populace. They would find out all during their rule that this was part of the price a conqueror had to pay if he remained among the people he had subdued.

Back in Paris, the empire builders were riding high. De la Grandière's coup had strengthened their position and their confidence. Things were going so well that it seemed nothing could go wrong. Then all of a sudden it did. Louis-Napoleon, who had a weakness for wars, became embroiled in a new one. This time, however, he made the mistake of taking on the rising state of Prussia which had the best army and the best generals in Europe.

Otto von Bismarck, Prussia's brilliant prime minister, had tricked Napoleon into declaring war. When the luckless Bonaparte fell into the trap he had set, Bismarck gave Europe its first taste of modern lightning warfare. The Germans invaded France on August 4, 1870. Less than one month later, on September 1, the two armies clashed in a major engagement at Sedan. This battle became for the ill-starred emperor what Waterloo had been for his uncle Napoleon. The victorious Prussians captured 100,-

000 French troops, as well as Napoleon himself. Although Paris, under siege, fought on heroically, the war's outcome was never in doubt. On January 28, 1871, the same day that Paris surrendered, the new French premier, Adolphe Thiers, signed an armistice agreement with Bismarck. France had suffered a severe setback in power, pride and prestige. It had also been forced to give Prussia its strategic border region of Alsace-Lorraine.

The war had upset the timetable of those who wished to see France become a great overseas empire. In the wake of defeat, colonies did not seem as important as they had before it. French politicians and patriots were now more intent on regaining Alsace-Lorraine than they were in embarking on additional adventures abroad. This mood, which persisted throughout the 1870s, made it difficult for the imperialists to get government backing for any new projects. If someone like Admiral Dupré, the new governor of Cochinchina, intended to make further conquests, he would have to do it strictly on his own. Which is exactly what the ambitious governor tried to do.

Now that they had the colony of Cochinchina, some Frenchmen there were ready to take the next step—conquest of the north—with or without the approval of Paris. That part of the country had been made to seem even more desirable by the results of a recent expedition up the Mekong River. One of the reasons that the French had begun their conquest of Vietnam in the south was their belief that its great waterway, the Mekong, would provide direct passage to the rich trade and markets of west China. In 1866, the minister of colonies, Chasseloup-Laubat, had commissioned a six-man team of explorers to find out if the Mekong led to China as everyone thought it did. The party was commanded by two naval officers, Captain Doudart de Lagrée and the young but audacious Francis Garnier. Two years later, five of the six men—minus Captain de Lagrée who had died of illness—returned to France to report on their perilous trip up this long, unexplored river. The Mekong, contrary to all expectations, did not go to China. Had the explorers continued on, instead of breaking off their journey, they would have wound up somewhere in the wild stretches of Tibet, a long way indeed from west China. The travelers told harrowing tales about the hardships that had hounded them every mile of the way. Leaving the tempestuous Mekong, they had worked their way by land and by water to China, and then, by sea, back to France.

The minister of colonies was disappointed to learn that the Mekong expedition had been a failure. But his interest was revived by some other news his explorers had brought. There *was* a river that went from China to Vietnam. This was the Red River of the north, in the domain still ruled by Tu Duc. A member of the expedition was to put it most graphically in an article he wrote later: "This way of communication searched for so fervently, this outlet through which we may one day expect the excess wealth of western China to flow into a French port—it is the Red River, not the Mekong." That turned matters squarely around. Control of the north now became the main goal of those who stood to profit the most from the China trade.

One such man was Jean Dupuis, a French trader who lived in the Chinese city of Hankow. He and Francis Garnier had met and talked when the latter visited Hankow in 1868. Dupuis had been extremely interested in the expedition's discovery that China could be reached from Vietnam via the Red River, and vice versa. Most of his business was in guns and other weapons of war, which now had to be transported by a long, difficult route over land. If what Garnier had told him were true, there was an easier and cheaper way to bring military goods into Yunan province. That would mean more business and more money for trader Dupuis, plainly a good thing.

Never a man to shy away from a challenge, the adventurous Dupuis decided to put Garnier's information to the test. He would make a voyage down the Red River to see if it could be navigated safely in a ship large enough to carry a commercial cargo. The first time he tried it, his expedition, which never got as far as the river itself, was driven back to Hankow by rebel bands. His second attempt, in 1870, encountered no such obstacle. From Yunan province, Dupuis sailed safely all the way to Hanoi. On his return trip he brought a big shipment of arms which he sold at a better profit than ever to the governor of Yunan, his best customer for such goods.

In 1873, Dupuis loaded some ships with tin and sailed to Hanoi again. When he prepared to make the return trip with an illegal cargo of salt, he was stopped and detained by Tu Duc's officials. Dupuis' answer was to order his heavily armed crew of 150 men to fight. This small but tough force seized part of Hanoi and sent word to Admiral Dupré in Saigon that it would hold out until help arrived. To the governor of Cochinchina this appeal should have come as a complete surprise—but it didn't. The action taken by Dupuis, historians later discovered, had all been part of a prearranged plan between the trader and governor. Dupré needed a good official reason for attacking the north, and Jean Dupuis had agreed to provide it.

Now that the first stage of his plan had been carried out, Dupré prepared the second stage. First, he told the government in France about the action taken by Dupuis and described it as a heaven-sent opportunity. Tu Duc's regime was tottering. This was the time to take Tonking and seize control of the Red River. All Paris had to do was give him the go ahead and he would act.

The French government ministers were well acquainted with Dupré's ideas about greater expansion in Vietnam. He had made himself very clear about that in a report he had written earlier that spring. "To establish ourselves in the rich country bordering on China," he wrote, "is a question of life and death for the future of our rule in the Far East." Paris had been just as opposed then to this idea as it was now. The government had made it plain to Dupré that he was not to engage in any unauthorized schemes. When it learned what Jean Dupuis had done in Hanoi, it sent instructions to the governor of Cochinchina not to involve France in this impetuous, dangerous escapade. But the communication from Paris reached Saigon too late to stop Dupré from taking positive action. A French force under the command of Francis Garnier, hero of the Mekong exploit, was already on its way to Hanoi.

Strange to say, it was Tu Duc himself who enabled Governor Dupré to go on with his scheme even if Paris were to object. After Jean Dupuis had established himself in Hanoi, Tu Duc asked Saigon to help him get rid of the French trader. This request gave Dupré the best excuse possible for taking matters into his own hands even without his government's permission. So it was as a friend who had come to render assistance that Francis Garnier was greeted when he arrived at the emperor's court in Hue.

The governor had made a shrewd choice in the man he picked to send north. Garnier's assignment was delicate and difficult, for it demanded that he be a master of intrigue as well as a captain of men. It seemed an odd role for this young Frenchman who was already famous as an explorer and scholar, but who had yet to make his mark as either diplomat or warrior. There was certainly no question about his great gifts of intelligence and courage. His massive, two-volume report on the Mekong expedition, recently published in Paris, had drawn high praise and was already considered a model of its kind; and, as the leader of that same epic journey, he had shown himself to be exceptionally resourceful. Now, at the age of thirty-four, having resigned from the navy, he was back in Asia to take up a private career as explorer and businessman. But Dupré's call to action had come like the summons of destiny. Garnier could not resist the lure of empire and glory. When he set out for Hanoi he had the governor's full authority behind him. Dupré had told him to act in any way he deemed necessary for the success of his mission, which was to rescue Dupuis and also to gain the use of the Red River for European ships. He was to accomplish this by negotiation, if possible, and by force, if necessary. To Francis Garnier his orders were clear. He would soon show how well he understood them by his use of the unlimited powers that the governor had given him.

His first move was to gain access to Dupuis' beleaguered force in Hanoi. This he did by assuring Tu Duc that he had come to help him get rid of the French trader, after which he would enter into peaceful negotiations with the Vietnamese about the use of the Red River. The emperor, though doubtful about Garnier's real intentions, decided to trust him. This error in judgment proved costly.

The perceptive Garnier had already taken note of Tu Duc's noticeable weakness. His army was small and ill-equipped, and the hostility of the people toward his regime was apparent to anyone with eyes and ears. To Garnier this was an open invitation to the use of force. Why negotiate when he could get what he wanted simply by taking it?

49

As soon as he and his men reached Hanoi, they teamed up with the jubilant Dupuis. Then Garnier held some inconclusive talks with Vietnamese officials about French use of the Red River. This, however, was just window-dressing for his real plans. Tu Duc's mandarins were hardly prepared for Garnier's next move. Completely on his own authority, he issued a proclamation which declared the Red River to be an international water route open to all foreign shipping. With this bold step, Garnier dropped the pose of peaceful negotiator. When his troops attacked and captured the citadel at Hanoi, the game was out in the open at last. Now his men fanned out into the surrounding countryside, destroying everything in their path. In a matter of weeks, his name had become a symbol of terror and ruthlessness to the Vietnamese. From October, 1873, when he arrived in Hanoi, to December of that same year, Francis Garnier ruled the valley area of the Red River like an oriental potentate. In the name of France, whose flag now flew over half of Tonking, he had become the scourge of the north. Then, as abruptly as it had begun, his career of conquest and violence ended. On December 21, the man who in his decrees called himself "the Great French Mandarin," was killed in action on the outskirts of Hanoi. In the person of this former naval officer, France had found —and then suddenly lost— its greatest soldier of empire in the East.

The dramatic manner of Garnier's death, in a fierce struggle with Chinese pirates, cast a romantic aura around his name and added to the formidable legend about him, which still exists. Actually, he was lucky to have died when he did; even as he fell outside Hanoi, forces were busy conspiring against him and his newly won empire. It was no secret, for instance, that his own government in France was most unhappy about his campaign in Tonking and wished he had never started it. What if the other European powers in Asia took Garnier's reckless bid for power as a general invitation for intervention in Vietnam? Just the thought of such a possibility made the Paris politicians shudder. Still licking its wounds from the Prussian war, France was anxious to avoid any incidents that might lead to conflict or cast it in a bad light.

Governor Dupré had also been encountering heated opposition in Saigon from those who felt that his militant

50

emissary had gone too far. Besides, why was the governor wasting his time with foolish adventures in the north when there was still much work to be done in the richer south? The grumbling and the criticism continued, and finally word came from Paris that the occupation of Tonking was to be brought to an end. The wily Dupré, caught in a crossfire of his antagonists at home and abroad, had a road of retreat ready. He informed his government that he had sent Garnier north for the sole purpose of forcing recognition by Tu Duc of all six French provinces in the south, something the emperor had never done officially. To prove his good faith in this regard, Dupré dispatched a new emissary to the court at Hue, a Monsieur Philastre who was also his most severe critic in Saigon of the Tonking adventure. This was a clever move, for there was no doubt in anyone's mind that Philastre wished to find a quick solution to the sorry mess.

Garnier was still reigning and acting like a king when Philastre departed from Saigon early in December, 1873. He went straight to Hue, where he and Tu Duc worked out an agreement satisfactory to them both. Then he proceeded to Hanoi to order the withdrawal of French forces and to restore both territory and government to Vietnamese hands. Garnier was already dead when Philastre arrived, but Jean Dupuis, the instigator of the affair, was still around. The French trader was summarily booted out of the country and sent back to China without his ships or cargo, light punishment indeed for so serious an offense.

So it was that what Garnier had won by the sword, Philastre signed away with the pen. In return, French Cochinchina—all of it—was finally given formal recognition by the Vietnamese. This was small consolation to Admiral Dupré who had been playing for bigger stakes and had lost. It was obvious, too, that Paris would be most unhappy if he continued in his present post, so the admiral submitted his resignation which, to no one's surprise, was accepted. Dupré, Dupuis and Garnier—these three names had only a short time before set Vietnam on fire. Now they were gone from the scene and the stage was ready for a fresh cast of characters.

New times bring new moods, new men and new policies. It took ten years for the mood of Paris to change from one of caution to open aggressiveness. This was part of a general attitude that was affecting all of Europe. Overseas expansion began to speed up as nations raced each other to see which would be the first to plant flags on new colonial territories. Those who had gotten a head start had already seized the choicer areas. Those who were new to the game—Germany, Belgium, Russia and Japan—went after the leftovers. The driving force behind this latest imperialist surge was the same that had impelled Europe in that direction earlier—a growing industrial society whose needs kept getting greater and greater.

In 1883, Jules Ferry became premier of France. He was an ardent believer in empire. "Colonial policy," he had written, "is the daughter of industrial policy." In an age of intense competition, France would either acquire colonies or she would become a third-rate power. Ferry, like many other Frenchmen who shared his feelings, was determined that this should not happen. In Vietnam, for instance, there was still some unfinished business. The order was given to complete it.

A new move against the north had already been made in the spring of 1882. Following in the footsteps of Francis Garnier, a young French officer named Captain Henri Rivière had attacked Hanoi and forced its surrender. Unlike Garnier, however, he had the full backing of his government. In a year's time he had brought lower Tonking under French control. Then in May, 1883, Rivière was killed, also, oddly enough, in an encounter with Chinese pirates outside Hanoi. When Paris heard the lamentable news about its conquering captain, it quickly sent more troops to finish the job he had begun. The army of Tu Duc had been unable to stop Rivière's six-hundred-man force. It was completely helpless against the added power which France now threw into the struggle.

The month of August witnessed the last act in the French drive for empire in Vietnam. Meeting little opposition, its soldiers took the rest of Tonking. With all of the north lost, further resistance by the Vietnamese was futile. On August 25, a treaty was signed which made Tonking and Annam, the central part of the country, French protectorates. All of Vietnam now belonged to France, thus bringing to a close the slow march of conquest that had begun twenty-five years before at Tourane.

The Emperor Tu Duc did not live to see the final subjugation of his country. He had died a month earlier, in July, in the bitter knowledge that he had failed. The hated Europeans would be masters of this ancient land. But now that they were its masters, they would have to hold it and rule it against a people whose whole history was a testament to its love of freedom. TuDuc's legacy, a defiant one, was announced to the people after his death. Their emperor, wrote the court mandarins in a proclamation, had been "killed by sorrow to see the foreigners invade and devastate his empire, and he died with curses against the invader on his lips. Keep him in your hearts and avenge his memory."

Chapter 4

FRENCH INDOCHINA

No sooner had the French been granted protectorate rights over Tonking and Annam than they found themselves at war with China, which also wanted a share of the spoils. The Chinese had invaded northern Tonking on the pretext of protecting its inhabitants from the French. What they really wanted, however, was a slice of Vietnamese territory near their own border. But the French would not let them have it without a fight. Since force seemed the only way to settle the dispute, the two parties fought it out for more than a year. Finally, the Chinese gave up their claim to part of Tonking. They signed the Treaty of Tientsin in 1885, which recognized French rule over the two new protectorates. The French also gained a little extra from their war with the Chinese—trading rights in the area of China bordering on Tonking.

Now that they had control of Vietnam, the French set about wiping out any traces of it as a single, unified country. Thus did Vietnam lose its freedom, its national identity and even its name. It became part of a larger complex of territories that the world would henceforth know as French Indochina. The official name given it—the Indochinese Union—was established by decree in 1887. This new territorial arrangement also included Cambodia and

54

Laos, the latter being added to the new Union as a protectorate in 1893.

Vietnam was split into three administrative units. Cochinchina remained the colony it had been since 1863. Annexed outright by France, it was ruled, as in the past, by a French governor. As a colony, however, Cochinchina had special status and privileges. It was allowed, for instance, to send representatives to the French legislature in Paris. Also, a Vietnamese living in Cochinchina could become a French citizen if he qualified. Tonking and Annam, on the other hand, enjoyed no such privileges; nor were they made part of France, though they were governed and administered by French officials.

The governmental structure of the protectorates differed slightly from each other. In Annam, the emperor and his mandarins were allowed to maintain a court at Hue, as before. But the chief French official of the protectorate, the résident supérior, was the real power in Annam. Tonking was also run by a résident supérior. To head the entire governmental structure of French Indochina, Paris created the new office of Governor-General. This man, whoever he might be, became, in effect, the most powerful figure in France's Asian empire.

On paper, French Indochina was a fact. But it was a long way yet from being a working reality. Just as it had in Cochinchina, the pattern of occupation now repeated itself in Tonking and Annam. Again, the French were to discover to their sorrow that military victory is but the first and easiest step of conquest. The real difficulty came afterward when the conquerors tried to govern. After twenty years of running Cochinchina, there was still guerrilla resistance. Now the same troubles began for the French in their new possessions. The Vietnamese had given Tu Duc and his mandarins lukewarm support in their fight against the French. That was because the people held the imperial regime responsible for their general poverty and misery. But as soon as the French took over, this wrath was turned against them, especially because they were foreigners.

How did the French meet this threat? Very simply. They initiated a policy of brutal suppression that was to turn their new empire into a slaughterhouse. Before the situation was brought under control, Indochina literally ran red with blood. Mandarins, as well as plain people, joined in the rebellious efforts against the French. Even the new boy emperor, Ham Nghi, and his court had taken part in an anti-French coup. This defection by the monarch in 1885 taught the French a lesson. In the future, no one sat on the throne unless he was handpicked and approved by Paris.

For more than twelve years, the French and the rebels engaged in a fight to the death, in which neither side gave quarter or showed mercy. During this period of resistance and revolt, Indochina, as one observer put it, was all "blood and fire." A French official, writing from the north in 1886, reported: "The capital was in our hands, but not even the surroundings were safe; the revolt triumphed everywhere; we had no friends, and even the people surrounding the king, who was our creature, were not in our favor."

The violence and the killing shocked many Frenchmen. While the bloodletting went on, it was impossible even to begin any of the long-range economic projects that were planned for Indochina. Such programs needed peace and the cooperation of the people. "It seemed to me," wrote one former governor-general, who had favored such an approach, "that the burning of villages, the mass shootings, the bayonet slaughters, and the execution of notables should be replaced by less violent procedures." They were, finally, but not until the last rebel bands had been driven into the mountains of the north where they still caused occasional trouble.

Only with the arrival in Indochina of Governor-General Paul Doumer in 1897, was a peaceful policy of reform finally started. Indochina had been pacified, but at a terrible cost that left scars for years afterward. The French, however, had established themselves firmly in power. It had required a campaign of repression and terror, but the French had proved one thing. They intended to stay and rule.

The changes introduced by the new rulers affected every aspect of Vietnamese life. Vietnam, with its ancient customs and traditions, underwent a radical transformation. With little warning or preparation, it was plunged headlong into modern times. For a people whose basic institutions hadn't changed since the twelfth century, it was like

56

being suddenly immersed in ice water. As the emperors had long known, the greatest danger from the West came not from its military might, but from its ideas: subversive doctrines they had tried to keep out by their unsuccessful policies of isolation. Now there was taking place that tragic meeting of cultures they had long feared, in which the old must bow before the new. Social relationships that had been stable for centuries began to shift and crack under the pressure of foreign ways.

First, the French shook up and destroyed the old governing apparatus of the country. As French officials took over, the power and influence of the royal family went into decline. The figurehead emperor still sat on the throne, but he had no real power. If he behaved himself, he was allowed to live in the palace at Hue and to maintain the fiction and trappings of royalty. If not, the French simply dismissed him and replaced him with someone more acceptable to them.

The mandarins, too, lost the great power they had once possessed. In times past, the examinations for the mandarinate had always attracted a great number of candidates. Gradually, these dropped almost to the vanishing point. One set of statistics serves to illustrate this decrease most vividly. In 1903, ten thousand people took the examinations for mandarins. By 1913, this figure had fallen to 1,-330.

As the old mandarin elite broke up, it was replaced by a new elite. This new group had abandoned the old Confucianist teachings. Its training, instead, was in modern subjects, such as science, history, medicine, and law, which it studied at schools established by the French. This was the French way of fulfilling what it called its "mission of civilization." France did not build too many of these schools, but the few it did build proved sufficient to spread the new ideas. From these institutions of learning, there came also those French-speaking Vietnamese who were employed in the lower echelons of the government civil service. Any Vietnamese who held or sought such a position had to learn the French language. Even members of old mandarin families who had been opposed to a French education began sending their children to French schools. The new education also had political effects. A rising generation began to understand that only by studying western ideas and techniques would it be able to offer effective opposition to the French.

Some Vietnamese were sent to France to study. There they saw the difference between the way a Frenchman behaved at home and the way he behaved in Indochina. They were also impressed by the noble tradition of Liberty, Equality and Fraternity, which had come out of the great French Revolution of 1789. These were dangerous ideas to put in the heads of impressionable young people who were itching to try them out in their native lands. Some Frenchmen were well aware of this and warned that a French education would have a corrupting influence on a Vietnamese student.

Schools in the villages of Vietnam also fell victim to change. Traditional Confucian subjects were dropped and modern ones put in their places. Reading and writing Chinese, and the use of Chinese ideographs in writing, were gradually abolished. Vietnamese boys and girls were now taught to read and write Vietnamese and French. This was a fatal blow to the Confucian scholar, once revered and respected for his knowledge. Like the mandarin, he, too, suffered a loss in influence and prestige.

In developing the economy of Indochina, the French made further innovations. They cleaned up the cities with systems of sanitation and hygiene. Their world-famous Pasteur Institutes sought cures for tropical diseases that had been plaguing the land for centuries. They also put down modern roads and constructed the impressive Trans-indochinese Railroad, which ran parallel to the old Chinese-built Mandarin Road, from Saigon in the south to the Chinese border in the north. French engineers also improved old ports, dredged out new ones, and helped tame rivers with dikes and irrigation projects.

Then there was the economy itself. The French began large-scale agriculture. New lands were opened to rice cultivation. Indochina had never been a rice-surplus area. Under the French, it was to rank third in the world as an exporter of rice. New crops were also brought in, most importantly, rubber and coffee. Tea, a native Vietnamese product, was exploited more successfully than it had ever been. Coal mines in Tonking became so productive that the French were soon able to export more coal than any other country in Southeast Asia. Other mines produced valuable quantities of tin, tungsten and zinc. Like most colonial countries, Indochina had few industries. The French built some cement plants and cotton mills. There was a scattering of other factories—tobacco, rice, glass, matches —and also some breweries. But these were the exceptions rather than the rule. Colonies were used mainly as markets for goods and as sources of raw material. The industrial nations of Europe and the United States had the factories that turned out the finished goods.

There were curious side effects of all this economic upsurge. One unlooked-for result, certainly, was the sudden, explosive growth of Chinese in the country. Foreign trade, whatever there was of it, was already being run by the Chinese when the French took over. Under the old imperial regime, there had been a ban on rice exports. When the French lifted this ban, Chinese merchants and shopkeepers came into Indochina in droves. In 1889, there were an estimated 57,000 Chinese living there. More began to come in when the French imported Chinese labor to help them build their new railroads and highways. By 1931, the number of Chinese in Indochina had risen to 217,000, an astonishing increase.

The Chinese became an important part of the economic life of Indochina. Most of them were engaged in trade and light industry. Others were bankers, craftsmen and shopkeepers. Few villages in the south, for instance, were without a Chinese shopkeeper. They also held a virtual monopoly over Indochina's rice mills and were prominent in the lumber and ship building industries. Many Chinese began their careers working on the new rubber plantations started by the French. Those who saved their money went into business for themselves, many as owners of tea and pepper plantations. Another interesting fact about this energetic and enterprising people—most of the fresh vegetables sold in Saigon today come from the gardens of Chinese farmers living in the suburbs of that city. They also own and operate many Saigon restaurants and hotels.

The boom in business and finance enriched a few within Indochina and sent huge profits back to investors in France. It also affected the lot of the average Vietnamese, but not in quite the same way. To finance their new ventures, the French needed more revenue. So they raised taxes. Hardest hit were the villages. Higher taxes squeezed them. Peasants were also forbidden to sell or trade in salt, opium or alcohol. The French established monopoly control of these commodities. They had previously supplied the peasant with other sources of income and he felt the loss most keenly.

The French reclaimed and developed vast new tracts of rice land. New canals and improved methods of irrigation and drainage added millions of fertile acres to the agricultural economy. A new class of huge estate owners came into being among the Vietnamese. Speculators bought up more and more land which they then rented or leased to tenant farmers. Many landowners moved to the cities where they could better spend their newfound wealth. This growing class of absentee landlords returned occasionally to collect rents and the interest due them on loans.

As the pattern of land ownership changed, a widening gulf opened up between rich and poor Vietnamese. The large landowners increased their holdings, while the share allotted to the peasant and his family grew smaller. The peasant stood at the very bottom of this edifice of greed and growing wealth. His daily life consisted of backbreaking toil and debt. He was in constant need of loans from the moneylender, who charged him outrageous interest rates. In Cochinchina, where most large estates were concentrated, the landlord often made more money from moneylending than he did from rent. About three quarters of the land in Cochinchina was worked by tenant farmers, or sharecroppers, as we call them. The peasant's contribution to the landlord was usually more than half his yearly harvest. Part of this paid his rent; the rest went to the moneylender.

There also took root, under the French, a social formation new to this ancient land—a Vietnamese working class, which sprang up with the growth of industries in the north. Landless peasants found their way into the factories and the mines. Others, mainly from Tonking, went south to work on the rubber plantations. Most workers who came from the villages thought that one day they would go back and become farmers again. But soon they came to understand that the change was a permanent one. When they realized this, they began to regard themselves as workers rather than as peasants. This growing class, with its special interests and problems, also had a disruptive effect on Vietnamese society.

That society, as time went on, was hard to recognize under the new surface of Indochinese life. Even the village, long the citadel of ancient ways, had undergone a fundamental transformation. Outwardly, it seemed the same, but appearances were deceptive. Most affected was the relationship between peasant and the mandarin aristocrat. In the old Confucian system, although separated by wealth and social position, there had nevertheless been a bond between them based on traditional obligations and responsibilities. Now those ties were severed. The peasant saw how certain mandarins cooperated with the French to further their own ends. From then on, he looked with suspicion and distrust at those who for the sake of profit and power had abandoned their moral heritage. Seeing the corruption and decay at the top levels of society, the peasant gradually lost his belief in the moral values of the past.

This breakdown in belief penetrated the entire fabric of society. Alienated from the French, as well as from their discredited old leaders, the people began to look elsewhere for leadership and for a solution to their problems. Thus was the way made open for a new phenomenon that would soon make the whole Asian continent tremble—nationalism. This new nationalism, in contrast to the old, would not seek merely to drive out the foreign master and restore the old order. Its aim was to create an entirely new order. The burning question then became: what kind of order would this new order be?

On one side was the huge mass of people, and on the other, the French and some favored few Vietnamese. A small middle class had also come into being under the French, and a group of white-collar workers which included secretaries, clerks, cashiers, interpreters, translators, and lesser government officials. These, too, had little power or influence. Even the very rich Vietnamese were cut off from the actual levers of political and economic power. The French exercised monopolistic control of industry and big business. French banks played a central role in the economy. Largest and most powerful of these financial institutions was the Bank of Indochina.

The French tried to mask their political supremacy by allowing some high-ranking mandarins to sit on councils and on other governing bodies, but the fiction deceived no one. All real authority belonged to the French and everyone knew it. To the educated Vietnamese, it had become clear that the best he could expect under the French was second-class citizenship. This was a situation he found intolerable at all levels of his experience—social, economic and political. Even if he had the same job as a European, he was paid less money for performing it. The French might have learned something from American colonial policy in the Philippines, where public service departments employed Filipinos on their staffs. In Indochina such positions were held by Frenchmen. One statistic may be instructive in this regard. To govern India, with its enormous population of over 350 million people, the British used under 5,000 civil servants. To govern Indochina, which had less than 30 million people, the French used more than 5,000 civil servants.

A Vietnamese in Indochina had few personal liberties. The French police and courts could act almost at will. A free press did not exist. It was easier, for example, for a Vietnamese to publish a newspaper in the French language than it was in his native tongue. The rights of assembly were limited and tightly controlled. Political parties were not allowed a formal legal existence, except in Cochinchina where the authorities kept a close watch on them. Trade unions were similarly banned. Freedom of travel was also restricted. Special permission had to be obtained to move from one region to another. And if a Vietnamese wished to go to France, he had to carry a police visa.

Such a system could hardly be loved or supported by those who lived under it. Many who worked for the French by day plotted their downfall at night. On the surface, life might appear peaceful. Below the surface, however, the seeds of revolt were slowly taking root.

Armed resistance in Indochina had never completely stopped. Even during relatively tranquil periods, agitation and demonstrations continued. Leading this unrest was a succession of patriotic parties and movements. Not until 1925 was the first communist group in Indochina organized by the Moscow-trained revolutionary, Ho Chi Minh. Before this important development, resistance to the French had been carried out solely by nationalists. The story of these groups and parties is really a history of political opposition in Indochina, which can be traced chronologically from the first nationalist stirrings after the French took over right up to modern times.

The first oppositionists were known as the Can Vuong, or Monarchist Movement. Its leaders were outstanding representatives of the traditional society who wished to bring back the old order. In the forefront of its ranks were the emperors themselves, the mandarins, generals and Confucian scholars. Mainly a movement of armed rebellion, it had its greatest strength during the period following 1885. Its decline was brought about by military defeat. The movement itself lingered until the year 1913 when it ceased to be a political factor.

In 1907, there appeared a new group that did important work for two years and then, having fulfilled its mission, also disappeared. This was the Dong Kinh Nghia Thuc, or "Private Schools" Movement, which was a delayed reaction to the impact of Western ideas and education. At first, most Vietnamese, steeped in the Confucian tradition, refused to send their children to the new French schools. This did not displease the French, who used them mainly to educate those Vietnamese they were training to become minor government officials. Later, however, when some scholars had read French books in, of all things, Chinese translations, they realized that they had been sadly in error. In these books they discovered that the French in Indochina had been keeping discreetly quiet about their great traditions of liberty and about such eminent French philosophers of freedom as Rousseau, Voltaire, and Montesquieu.

Now, those who had been sending their children to the old Confucianist schools began sending them instead to the French schools. There weren't enough schools, however, to meet the increased demand, and the Vietnamese began to agitate for more. The French were slow to comply, so the Vietnamese began to build their own private schools which taught Western ideas. The French shut down these schools and imprisoned those who were behind the new movement.

The scholars fought back by organizing demonstrations that demanded lower taxes as well as the reform of the educational system. Some of these demonstrations did have positive results. The French built more schools, including the University of Hanoi, which opened in 1918. Such action by the French encouraged some scholars to believe that it might now be possible to cooperate with the Europeans and achieve their objectives by peaceful means. Their aim was a simple one—a modern country with democratic political institutions.

Another group, which had come into existence in 1905, two years before the Private Schools crusade, was the Dong Du, or Pan-Asian Movement. The scholars in this movement did not share the viewpoint of the Private Schools leaders. They doubted that collaboration with the French was possible. Only through the force of arms, they believed, could they win their national freedom and set about modernizing the country. They were greatly inspired by the victory of Japan over Russia in 1905. Their brilliant leader, Phan Boi Chau, sought help for his movement in other Asian lands. He traveled to Japan and China in the hope that he could interest nationalist leaders there in the cause of Vietnamese independence. He became a friend and associate of China's Dr. Sun Yat Sen and other important Asian nationalists.

Despite reverses, Phan Boi Chau was making his greatest progress at the very moment he was arrested by the French police in Shanghai in 1925. Phan was sent back to Indochina where he was tried and subsequently sentenced to be beheaded. But after great public protest, Phan's sentence was rescinded and he was granted an amnesty. Thereafter, he was kept under house arrest in Hue and died on October 20, 1940. His movement, which had been centered mainly around his dynamic leadership, declined after his arrest and vanished altogether with his death.

The nationalist movements described so far were the work of men who came out of the old traditionalist society. Most of them had been born before the French came to Indochina, so that there was a big gap in both age and attitudes between them and members of the younger generation. This new generation, which had been educated in French schools and nurtured on Western ideas, also began to involve itself in nationalist politics.

One of this new breed, Nguyen Thai Hoc, became the leader of the first modern nationalist movement of Indochina. Organized informally at first, in 1925, most of its members were small tradesmen, minor government officials, white-collars workers, and army officers serving with the native Indochinese troops. In 1927, the young militants opened up a publishing house in Hanoi and began printing political tracts. The new publishers were quickly closed down by the police. After this setback, Nguyen Thai Hoc and his friends formed a real political organization, the Viet-Nam Quoc-Dan Dang, or Nationalist Party of Vietnam, more popularly known by its initials, VNQDD. Their model was the famous Kuomintang party of China, which had been founded in 1912 by the illustrious Dr. Sun Yat Sen.

Nguyen Thai Hoc organized his party into two sections. One, the legal party, operated in public. The other section functioned secretly as an underground organization. This tactic proved very successful. By the early part of 1929, the combined sections had some 1,500 members, many of them military men. Well satisfied with their party's progress, its leaders were looking forward to even greater growth. Then unforeseen events forced the hand of the VNQDD and provoked it into a premature uprising.

In 1929 a French settler was murdered. The French police suspected the VNQDD of being behind the assassination. Many of its members were arrested and sent off to the dreaded camp for political prisoners on Poulo Condore Island. Nguyen Thai Hoc now feared that his secret section was in danger of being ferreted out and destroyed. To forestall this, preparations were made for a general uprising. The attack was to take place on February 10, 1930. This date was then changed to February 15, but the military garrison of Yen Bay, on the Chinese border, which was involved in the prospective rebellion, failed to receive word about the change. On February 10, as planned, it rose up in revolt. This premature uprising was a disaster. The rebellion was crushed and the VNQDD itself was smashed. Most of its members were arrested or executed. Nguyen Thai Hoc and twelve other leaders died on the guillotine. A lucky few escaped and fled to China where they tried to reestablish their party. But the VNQDD never regained its former influence. Its place was now taken by a brand-new organization that had just appeared on the political scene, the Indochinese Communist Party.

That party, which would one day make the revolution

against France, was the creation of a remarkable man named Ho Chi Minh. The history of Vietnamese communism and the life and career of this legendary Marxist revolutionary are inseparably intertwined. Therefore, we shall tell their stories as one.

Chapter 5

COMMUNISM AND HO CHI MINH

THERE are many gaps, contradictions and puzzling omissions in the life of the man known as Ho Chi Minh. In the first place, that is not his real name. During his early years as a communist, Ho used many aliases and pseudonyms. Ho Chi Minh is but the latest of these. It means, literally, "Ho who enlightens." His name, however, is not the only odd thing about him, as consider the following. An Asian, he was sent into Asia to stir up trouble by the Russian communists, whose agent he was. Although he was the undisputed leader of communism in Vietnam, he directed its affairs from afar. Only under conditions of war and conspiracy in 1940 did he finally return to the native land he hadn't seen in thirty years. As if this isn't strange enough, there were also rumors that he had worked, at times, for the French and British police. And—the final bizarre touch—when he reappeared in public in 1945, he was supposed to have been dead since 1933! This fact had even been reported as news in an English communist newspaper.

Ho's story, although certainly different in detail, is not unlike that of other Asian intellectuals who could not find places for themselves in their own societies. Communism, when it came to Asia, appealed to many such men. It offered power and leadership to those with education and ambition. It promised racial equality to people who had been made to feel racially inferior. It was also, in colonial countries, fervently nationalistic. Their professed patriotism gave communists stature in the eyes of other nationalists. In Asia, except for its vaguely understood economic doctrines, communism was viewed as just one more species of nationalism. This public image helped Ho build his organization. Posing as an ardent nationalist, which, in truth, he was, too, Ho was able to recruit followers who otherwise would not have joined him.

Communism, it should be noted, is a Western idea. It was brought into Asia from the outside, partly by Europeans and partly by Asians who first went to the West to study and learn it. The idea was actually as old as human society itself, but its modern version had been born in the brain of a nineteenth century German scholar, Karl Marx. This theory—called communism or socialism, interchangeably—had a simple premise. It was, in brief, that the new industrial market system of the West—capitalism— was a social evil. It led to the struggle of class against class and man against man. It exploited farmers and workers, made great depressions, and gave riches to the few and poverty to the many. To replace it, Marx suggested a new system—socialism. In the Marxian scheme, private ownership of the means of production would vanish. Land and industry would be owned by the state and the good things of life would be distributed on a more just basis. Eventually, even the state would disappear and men would work and live together in perfect harmony and human brotherhood.

When Marx lived and wrote, capitalism was still in its infancy. Marx predicted that as it grew older it would become sick with crisis and die. Its machines would produce so many goods that no one would be able to buy them all. Society would be divided up into a small number of rich capitalists and an overwhelming number of poor. Then the whole unwieldy system would break down. The huge army of poor would revolt and overthrow the ruling capitalists. Led by the socialists, they would then remake society based on communist principles.

In Europe, these ideas caused much consternation and dismay on the part of those who felt menaced by them. Socialist parties attracted many followers. As the first World War began in 1914, every country on the continent had a socialist or a labor party. There were still no communists, as we know them today. Most socialist parties, although they followed Marx, were basically democratic. They wished to do away with capitalism but their programs called for free political institutions.

The picture changed in 1917. In February, the war-weary Russians deposed the czar and established a democratic government. This binge of freedom was exhilarating but brief. In October, a coup d'etat by the Bolshevik party, led by Vladimir Ilyich Lenin, carried it to power in Russia. Lenin and his Bolsheviks throttled the Russian democracy and put a one-party dictatorship in its place. To set themselves apart from other socialist parties, they called themselves communists. The new Communist party of Russia had several basic goals. One was to bring about communism in Russia. Another was to form communist parties elsewhere by splitting the other socialist parties (mainly in Europe). The Russian communists also began to promote world revolution by means of a new international organization which they created—the Communist International.

Communist propaganda began to spread all over the globe. Its agents worked tirelessly to sow the seeds of revolt and win new members to their cause. Wherever there was misery and unrest, they found fertile ground for their work. The colonial world, seething with tensions and poverty, was made to order for revolutionaries. Before long, communist agitators were haranguing the masses of Asia, calling on them to rise up against the Europeans. One of them—an organizer rather than an agitator—was Ho Chi Minh.

The life of this mystery man of Asia begins, as might be expected, with another riddle. Was he born in 1890, 1891 or 1892? All three have been variously given as the year of his birth. We still do not know for sure, although the earliest date is the one now generally accepted. The North Vietnamese government lists it officially as May 19, 1890. For a long time even Ho's real name was not known. Now it has narrowed down to a choice between two—Nguyen That Thanh or Nguyen Van Thanh. You may, of course, take your pick.

His father, Nguyen Sin Huy, was a minor mandarin official with the imperial regime in central Vietnam. Ho's birthplace was the village of Kim-Lien, where, presumably, his brother Khiem and sister Thanh were also born. Nothing was known about these two older children until after Ho's ascension to power. Both took part in nationalist politics, but neither ever played more than a minor role. Brother Khiem's death occurred in 1950, and sister Thanh's in 1953.

At one point in his career, Ho's father lost his government job. His political beliefs were obviously the cause for his dismissal. Vehemently anti-French, he was a secret member of several nationalist groups. He made it easier for the authorities to fire him by refusing to learn French, which was then required of Vietnamese officials. All evidence points to the fact that the male parent of Ho espoused strong nationalist sentiments and that his youngest son was greatly influenced by those opinions. Ho must have been deeply impressed, for the story is told that, as a mere boy of nine, he was already acting as a messenger for the nationalist groups to which his father belonged.

Eventually, the family moved to South Vietnam, or, as it was then still called, Cochinchina. For some reason, very little is known about Ho's mother, who figures as a gray, scarcely visible blur against the backdrop of his early years. No items of any interest have come to light about her, nor has Ho ever spoken or written about her. There are additional areas of obscurity. It is not even known, for instance, if Ho ever married or had children. Conflicting stories still persist about this aspect of his life. Some sources say that he had once taken a wife in Russia; others maintain that he had not.

Ho was a student at the Lycée Quôc-Hoc in Hue, which had the reputation of being the best high school in Indochina. This school was most important in shaping Ho's mind, for it was here that he came to know other revolutionary students. Many of Vietnam's future nationalist and communist incendiaries passed through this same institution of learning. Two outstanding communist leaders, who today share power with Ho, also went to the Hue high school—Vo Nguyen Giap and Premier Pham Van Dong. Another student, who was not attracted to communism, was Ho's future great adversary, Ngo Dinh Diem, first president of South Vietnam.

Ho did not finish his schooling at Hue. His anti-French activities are said to have been responsible for his leaving. It is not known if he was expelled or left voluntarily under pressure. For a few years, he drifted about, working at various jobs. Then he decided to leave Vietnam and go to France. The departure occurred, probably, in 1912, although even that date is uncertain.

The young emigrant worked his way across the seas as a kitchen boy aboard a French ship. It was then that he assumed his first alias. The name he chose was Ba. The new kitchen boy got a real taste of travel and foreign ports. He saw colorful cities like Marseilles and the exotic west coast of Africa. His ship also beat its way up and down the North American continent.

Then came World War I in 1914. Ho gave up the sea and went to live in London. During the day he shoveled snow and in the evening he worked at the fashionable Carlton Hotel as a cook's helper. The greatest chef of that period, Escoffier, was Ho's boss in the Carlton's kitchen. Escoffier took a liking to the youthful Vietnamese and Ho soon rose to a favored position in the pastry section. During his stay in London, he naturally associated with fellow Asians and became a member of the Overseas Workers Association which, led mostly by Chinese, had an anti-colonialist program.

As the war dragged on, Ho decided to go to sea again. One of his journeys, it is said, took him to the United States, where he lived for a while in New York's Harlem. There he saw racial prejudice in action and was much impressed by the sights, sounds and size of the great city. When he returned to France, the war was entering its final year. Ho made his living retouching photographs.

The end of the war stirred hope in the hearts of many colonial peoples who saw in Woodrow Wilson's famous Fourteen Points a promise of freedom for their countries. To Versailles, where the Great Powers sat down to draft a treaty that would decide the fate of Europe and the world, there also came a stream of political lobbyists to plead their special causes. Twenty-eight-year-old Ho, wearing a rented dress suit and a bowler hat, was among those who came to Versailles for this purpose. He presented a written request for an audience, but it was never granted. Ho, then primarily a nationalist, wished to discuss his eight-point program for Vietnam, which was so mild that it did not even ask for independence. But the leaders at Versailles were too busy settling the big questions, so the so-called little questions never got the attention they merited.

Ho joined the French Socialist party at just about the time it was in the throes of a violent internal debate. The issue centered around the question of whether or not the party should affiliate itself with the new Communist Third International, or Comintern, as it was popularly called. In 1920, Ho attended the party congress at Tours as a delegate. During the debate on the main question—whether to leave the socialist Second International and join the Comintern—Ho made his position quite clear. In his statement, the only one he made at the congress, he revealed what his paramount concern was in choosing one course over the other:

"I don't understand a thing about strategy, tactics, and all the other big words you use, but I understand very well one single thing: The Third International concerns itself a great deal with the colonial question. Its delegates promise to help the oppressed colonial peoples to regain their liberty and independence. The adherents of the Second International have not said a word about the fate of the colonial areas."

This, for Ho, was the overruling issue, and he cast his ballot in favor of joining the communists. The socialists then split, one wing staying with the old party, the other going off to found a separate communist party. Ho was one of the charter members of this new communist organization. This formally began his career as a professional communist, a career that—at this moment of writing—has endured for some forty-six years. Ho soon reached a high place in party circles. Although not really one of its leaders, he did become its spokesman on colonial questions and edited a newspaper exclusively devoted to this subject.

He apparently went to Moscow to attend some of the early congresses of the Communist International, where he met the luminaries of the communist world, among them Lenin himself. Early in 1924, Ho made another trip to Moscow, this time for an entirely different purpose. Now, as a student at communist schools, he began an intensive study of Marxist teachings. This was also the period when Joseph Stalin and Leon Trotsky were struggling for supremacy inside the Russian party. Ho avoided taking sides in this political duel; he probably had no real interest in it, anyway. At any rate, by staying clear of it, he managed to survive all of the many Stalinist purges that decimated the communist ranks in later years.

Ho never fancied himself as a great scholar or writer, but he did write several pamphlets, one of which, *French Colonialism on Trial,* made him famous. This pamphlet was written under the pseudonym by which Ho was then best known in Vietnam—Nguyen Ai Quoc, which means "Nguyen, the patriot." Smuggled into Indochina, the pamphlet became the most important work—one can almost say the bible—of the Vietnamese nationalist movement, and the name of Nguyen Ai Quoc came to be revered by all patriots. Ho, or Nguyen Ai Quoc, in those days was looked upon as a genuine nationalist by his compatriots—a political disguise that was to fool many people along the way. While in Moscow, Ho's hatred of the French, which had been intense enough before his Russian tour, now became greater than ever. A new pen name began to appear at the bottom of the articles he wrote: Nguyen-O-Phap, or "Nguyen, who hates the French." As can readily be seen, each one of Ho's new names was politically inspired and served a political purpose. But this latter name was too strong even for the communists, and he was advised officially to drop it.

So far, Ho had been an apprentice at revolution, a student and propagandist learning his trade. Now he was ready to see active service on the political fronts of the world. His bosses at the Comintern had the perfect assignment for an Asian revolutionary—Asia. China in 1924 was beginning to rumble with revolution. It was there that the two major political forces of the twentieth century met head-on for the first time—nationalism and communism. On command of Moscow, the Chinese communists had formed a shaky alliance with the Chinese nationalists of the Kuomintang party. To guide their Chinese comrades in political and military matters, the Russians dispatched some of their top agents to China. Chief of this group was the redoubtable and legendary Michael Borodin. In those early, tumultuous days, Borodin was the Comintern's number-one revolutionary trouble-shooter. In China, he took command of the communist offensive and began to direct its strategy. Ostensibly, he was the head of something called the Russian Political Mission. This public front enabled him to work behind the scenes at the real job Moscow had sent him to do—make a revolution in China.

One of the members of Borodin's staff at the Russian Mission was Ho Chi Minh. Officially, he was listed as an interpreter. The Russians had their headquarters in the city of Canton. It was here that Ho began putting together his own organization of Vietnamese revolutionaries. Made up of political exiles living in China, it was formally named the Vietnamese Revolutionary Youth Association. Another of Ho's creations was the League of Oppressed Peoples of Asia, which had members from Malaya, India, China, Korea, Indonesia and Vietnam. This out-and-out communist front group later developed into the Communist Party of the South Seas, which was a kind of catchall communist organization for Southeast Asia. It lost both its function and its identity when the Southeast Asian countries began to form individual communist parties.

Ho proved himself an efficient organizer. The Vietnamese he trained and instructed in Canton were sent into Indochina where they became the nucleus of a growing communist movement. Ho also made practical use of the alliance between the Chinese communists and Chiang Kai-shek's Kuomintang. Chiang had a military academy at Whampoa where his own officers were trained by Russian officers under the command of General Bleucher, the foremost Soviet military specialist in China. Some of Ho's most able cadres were permitted to take the course at this academy, which gave them a thorough grounding in military strategy and tactics.

Every three months or so, Ho was able to send back to Indochina between twenty and thirty revolutionaries who had been specially indoctrinated by him. If he had doubts about any of his followers, there was a quick, effective way of getting rid of them. They were sent back to Indochina with the others, but while they were on their way their names were leaked to the French police who had no difficulty in picking them up after they crossed the border.

Ho also disposed of political opponents in the same way. He is reliably reported, for instance, to have been involved in the betrayal of Phan Boi Chau to the French police in 1925. This leader of Vietnam's nationalist Pan-Asian Movement, who was discussed in the previous chapter, was arrested just inside the French Concession in Shanghai. The sum paid to Ho by the French for this act of treachery is said to have been 100,000 paisters, a huge sum of money when one considers that five piasters at that time would purchase a water buffalo.

Phan's betrayal was arranged with the assistance of one of his close associates, Lam Duc Thu. It was this unsavory individual with whom Ho was supposed to have shared the money. The 50,000 piasters—the half which went to Ho—helped finance his new organization in Canton. Lam Duc Thu, on the other hand, did not waste his 50,000 on politics. He spent most of it in Hong Kong's night clubs and other places of pleasure.

Why did Ho betray Phan Boi Chau to the French? His communist followers gave three reasons. First, Ho thought that Phan, grown too old, had outlived his usefulness to the revolution. Second, he believed that Phan's arrest and trial would cause great indignation in Vietnam and arouse patriots to even greater revolutionary efforts. The third reason was financial. The money Ho got from the French would be used to build the movement and attract new recruits. The case of Phan Boi Chau is one outstanding instance of the communist tactic of betraying political rivals to the police. There would be others in the future.

In 1927, the alliance between the Chinese communists and the Kuomintang split wide open. Chiang Kai-shek's soldiers were given orders to exterminate communists on sight and a wholesale bloodbath followed. Ho and other Comintern agents were forced to flee the country. Little is known about his activities over the next few years. He is supposed, after having fled Canton, to have somehow made his way across the Gobi Desert back into the Soviet Union. His movements thereafter are obscure. There are stories that he worked in Berlin during this interval, that he attended a communist meeting in Brussels, and that he also paid secret visits to Switzerland and fascist Italy. He also became a Soviet citizen, something that most leading communists did who lived in Russia, no matter what their national origin.

In the late 1920's, Ho turned up again in the Far East, in Thailand, where he set up his headquarters. He shaved his head and pretended to be a Buddhist priest. In this disguise, he went safely about his subversive business among a large colony of Vietnamese refugees. While Ho was busy mixing religion with communism, his comrades back in Vietnam were in the midst of a fierce political fight. Three factions, which had opposing ideas about communist tactics, had split off from each other and formed rival organizations. Their open quarrel had made it easy for the French police to single out their members and arrest them. The dispute was threatening to destroy Vietnamese communism.

In Thailand, Ho received instructions from the Comintern to put an end to the division. Amazingly, he did just that. Leaders of the three groups were summoned to Hong Kong where they met with Ho to discuss the rift. The site of one of their meetings was, of all places, the bleachers of a soccer stadium. The talks went on for three weeks. Finally, Ho, whose powers of persuasion must have been great, got all the parties to iron out their disagreements and consent to the formation of a single communist organization embracing all three factions. The Communist Party of Vietnam, which came out of this conference on February 3, 1930, was later enlarged to include Cambodia and Laos and had its name changed to the Indochinese Communist Party.

Back in Vietnam, the new party immediately began to gain strength and influence. It was helped in this, of course, by the failure of the VNODD uprising at Yen Bay in 1930. The destruction of the leading nationalist party left the field wide open to the communists. Workers, students and intellectuals in the cities flocked to their banner. The communists also extended their operations into the countryside, where they claimed the support of 100,000 peasants through peasant organizations which they controlled.

The year 1930 was a year of terror. A widespread famine had brought demonstrations and appeals from the starving peasants. In the forefront of this peasant agitation were the communists. Labor unions were illegal but they organized them nevertheless. They even set up their own soviets—or councils—in two provinces of Annam. Peas-

76

ants attacked landlords and forcibly seized and divided up large estates. The French response to all this was quick and harsh suppression.

As the year drew to a close, the wheels of French justice ground swiftly. People were arrested, tried and convicted by the hundreds. There were no formal trials. The accused were simply brought before criminal commissions which needed no evidence to render judgment. The French Foreign Legion was used to hunt down suspects in the north and central parts of Vietnam. During this period of terror, thousands perished, the innocent as well as the guilty. But the reprisals, from the French point of view, had accomplished their purpose. They had crushed a budding revolution and restored order in the country.

After this, most revolutionary activity shifted to the south. Saigon, in Cochinchina, became the center of the new ferment. Communists, Trotskyites and other leftists were allowed a certain degree of leeway by the authorities, which even extended to the publication of newspapers. In 1932, the parties of the left actually elected two of their candidates—one Stalinist and one Trotskyite—to the Saigon municipal council. As time went on, left groups in the north once more began to engage in cautious, peaceful political agitation. The new tactic proved most effective and led to a network of cells throughout the land.

In 1936, the Popular Front came to power in France. While out of power, the French leftists had proclaimed anti-colonialist sentiments. It was a different matter, however, when this coalition of Socialist, Radical Socialist and Communist parties took over the reins of government. There were practical matters to consider. Europe was in the grip of a great depression and income from the colonies was sorely needed. The French people would have thrown out any regime that dared recommend freedom for the colonies.

But the Popular Front did improve conditions somewhat in Indochina. It removed a highly unpopular governor-general. There was also an amnesty for political prisoners. The end for the Popular Front came in 1938, when its government fell. In September, 1939, France, now at war with Germany, outlawed its own pro-Soviet Communist party. It also outlawed its counterpart in Indochina, thus driving it underground.

To the outsider, as the war years began, Indochina appeared relatively peaceful and quiet. The naked eye could certainly detect no signs of political unrest. As far as one could tell, the head of the revolution had been lopped off and rendered harmless. But looks were deceiving. Beneath the calm of public life, revolutionary forces of all shades and persuasions were regrouping and waiting patiently for the moment to strike.

What was Ho Chi Minh up to while all this was happening? For one thing, as was stated earlier, he was supposed to have died in 1933, according to reports which filtered out, after his arrest by the British in Hong Kong. The seizure of Ho had occurred in the following way.

In the spring of 1930, an important Comintern agent fell into the hands of the British police in Singapore. Usually such agents could be trusted not to reveal any vital information, but this one cracked under questioning and told all he knew. His revelations led to the arrest of key communists all over Southeast Asia, where the police, whether French, Dutch or Chinese, had been tipped off by the British. In Hong Kong, Ho was caught in the dragnet. He was arrested on June 5, 1931. Released from prison at the beginning of 1932, he dropped out of sight for several years. This void in his past is still unexplained. Some authorities believe that he was working as an agent for British Intelligence during this period. As proof, they point to his relatively mild six-month sentence, which is, allegedly, the price the English paid to get his cooperation. No one knows, of course, if this is true, but the mere fact that there have been other such assertions about Ho—about his relations with the British, the French, and even the Americans during World War II—adds credibility to these informed guesses, even though they remain unproven.

In 1934, we find Ho back in Moscow, his career, according to some, in temporary eclipse. He did some further studying at party schools and bided his time while he waited for another assignment. Stalin's purges of Russian and other communists were then getting under way, but Ho was in the fortunate minority that was spared the executioner's bullet or imprisonment in a concentration camp.

The year 1938 saw Ho off again, this time to China. There he served in various capacities with the communist forces of Mao Tse-tung, first with the communist 8th

Route Army, then with a special mission that was training Chinese nationalist guerrillas. He still kept in touch, of course, with the Indochinese communists, and in December, 1940, Ho re-entered Vietnam after an absence of thirty years. There, in the spring of 1941, he attended an important meeting of the central committee of the Indochinese Communist Party, whose decisions were to affect the future course of Vietnamese history. His return was significant. This communist man of the shadows, this flitting, wraithlike figure of many aliases and disguises was about to come out into the open. Great events were impending. Soon the whole world would know the name of Ho Chi Minh.

Chapter 6

END OF AN EMPIRE

T HE fall of France in 1940 was to set the stage for the fall of French Indochina. Nazi Germany's invasion of Poland in 1939 brought World War II to Europe after an uneasy peace of twenty years. Snug and secure behind its vaunted Maginot Line, France felt safe. But the Germans did not attack directly. Instead, they outflanked the impregnable French defense system and sliced into France by way of the Low Countries, Belgium and the Netherlands. Swift-moving panzer divisions cut the unprepared French forces to ribbons. The musty strategy of the French General Staff was straight out of World War I. It could not cope with the lightning-fast tactics of Hitler's mobile legions. The Germans had begun their drive on May 10, 1940. On June 14, they entered Paris. On June 22, an armistice was signed. France was defeated and humiliated. A new French government—remembered by history as the Vichy Regime because it established its capital at Vichy—took office under the aged Marshal Henri Philippe Pétain. From then until the end of the war in 1945, France lived under German occupation.

In Indochina, French officials, civilians and soldiers suddenly found themselves cut off from the home country. They were now on their own and could expect no help from the doddering Pétain and his semi-fascist government. This gave Japan the opportunity it had been waiting for. Already at war with China, the Japanese had even greater ambitions in Southeast Asia. General Tojo and his militarists regarded Indochina, with its favorable position on the Indochinese Peninsula, as the steppingstone into Southeast Asia. Control of its territory would put Japan within invasion range of Malaya, Burma, the Dutch East Indies, and even the Philippines. It also bordered on China and had a common frontier in the west with Thailand. Just as important, if not more so, were its rice and raw materials which could help feed and supply the hungry Japanese war machine.

Japan had another very good reason for wanting Indochina. Valuable war supplies were going up to Chiang Kai-shek in China via the Transindochinese Railroad. This had long been a sore point with the Japanese whose planes had even strafed and bombed a China-bound supply train earlier in April. So it was with interest and pleasure that they watched France fold up under the German spring blitz in Europe. Five days after Hitler's troops took Paris, on June 19, Japan issued an ultimatum to the governor-general of Indochina, General Georges Catroux.

The very next day General Catroux bowed to the Japanese demands. A brief, bloody battle between French and Japanese troops had made it clear that it would be suicidal to resist. The French had fought bravely but they had been badly outnumbered. So Catroux capitulated. He had very little choice. Earlier, knowing what was coming, he had asked the British and Americans for help. This had been refused. Both Anglo-Saxon powers hoped that if they kept a hands-off policy, Japan would not move. They were wrong. When Japan struck, it was too late for them to do anything about it.

The Japanese won military and, later, economic control of Indochina. But they still allowed French officials to run the country. French soldiers and police were also free to put down native uprisings, which still broke out from time to time. Japan even turned aside when the French crushed a rebellion led by pro-Japanese nationalists.

Ho Chi Minh, in the meanwhile, was laying his own plans. He realized that he now had two enemies to combat —Vichy France and Japan. To fight them both, he would have to seek wider political support. When the communists gathered for an important conference at the town of Pac-Bo, near the Chinese border, leading nationalists were invited to attend. On the last day of the meeting, May 19, 1941, a new organization was formed—the Viet Nam Doc Lap Dong Minh, or League for the Independence of Vietnam. This was soon shortened to Viet Minh, the name by which it became generally known. The communist-led coalition issued a manifesto that called on the Vietnamese people to wage unremitting struggle against the Japanese and French. Ho was elected secretary-general of the Viet Minh.

It was at this time that Ho assumed the name by which he has been known ever since, Ho Chi Minh. He had a good reason for doing so. The Viet Minh was supposed to be a patriotic organization. Ho wanted to hide the fact that its leader was the well-known communist, Nguyen Ai Quoc. Besides, Nguyen Ai Quoc was thought to have died long ago of tuberculosis. Ho's appearance had changed considerably over the years, which would make it easier for him to pretend he was someone else. So it was that, for the umpteenth time in his chameleon-like career, Ho literally became reborn by adopting a new alias. Not many knew, except for a few leaders in his own party, that Ho Chi Minh and Nguyen Ai Quoc were the same person. Even after he took power, Ho kept up the mystery about his identity. Only recently did he finally acknowledge that he was indeed the same Nguyen Ai Quoc whose deeds had made him a Vietnamese legend.

Under Ho, the Viet Minh became strong and popular. It also began making military preparations. Several of Ho's more able assistants, among them the brilliant Vo Nguyen Giap, were sent to work and study with Mao Tse-tung's communist armies. Ho himself was in charge of training guerrillas at a camp near the Chinese border.

Chiang Kai-shek and his Chinese nationalists watched Ho's activities warily. They were suspicious of the Viet Minh because so many of its leaders and followers were communists. Chiang had had long and bitter experience with communists in China. Even now, though they were supposed to be allies in the common fight against Japan, the nationalists and communists spent just as much time fighting each other as they did the Japanese. The Chinese leader knew that just as soon as the Japanese were beaten he would have to subdue the armies of Mao Tse-tung if he wished to rule all of China.

Chiang was not opposed to all Vietnamese revolutionaries—just the communists. Non-communist rebels received his warm support. They were, after all, fighting his own enemy, Japan; also, as an Asian, he wanted to see French power broken in Indochina. So the Chinese helped nationalists of all stripes with money and expert guidance. A training camp had even been set up for them in China, which was financed by a subsidy of $100,000 a month. The Viet Minh—many of whose members were nationalists—also benefited from this arrangement. But the Chinese kept a sharp eye on Ho Chi Minh, whom they did not fully trust. Finally, on one of Ho's trips into China, the nationalists arrested him. For more than a year, he was imprisoned in one of Chiang's jails. He was finally released on September 14, 1943. It is believed, on good authority, that Chiang let him go after the American Office of Strategic Services (OSS) in China intervened in his behalf. The Viet Minh was aiding the Allies in various ways. Its guerrillas were harassing the Japanese and helping downed American airmen escape. It was also supplying valuable intelligence reports. The OSS thought the Viet Minh would be even more effective with its leader out of jail. The Chinese were reluctant to turn Ho loose but finally gave in.

Ho went back to Vietnam. There he found his Viet Minh strongly entrenched in the mountains north of the Red River. Vo Nguyen Giap, also back from China, was busy organizing a guerrilla army. The Viet Minh did not conduct major guerrilla operations against the Japanese. But it was getting itself ready for the showdown, if and when it came. As the year 1945 began, Giap had ten thousand guerrillas trained and under arms.

In March, 1945, Japan suddenly seized control of Indochina. Ever since the liberation of France in the spring of 1944, the Japanese had been watching the French closely. Now that they were losing the war in Southeast Asia—at an ever faster rate—they were afraid that their erstwhile partners might turn on them. Lately, there had been increasing signs that the Free French underground in Indochina was getting ready to take up arms openly against them. The Japanese were worried that if the Free French went into action, the regular French troops might join forces with them. So Japan's military leaders decided to move first.

Without warning, on March 9, Japanese troops surrounded the French garrisons, then attacked. The French fought back but had no chance. Those who surrendered were disarmed. Some lucky few managed to break through and escape to China. Japan then proclaimed the independence of Vietnam. The young Emperor Bao Dai was asked to form a government. Bao Dai did as the Japanese requested. He called on the well-known scholar, Tran Trong Kim, to become premier. For the first time since the nineteenth century, the country was free of French rule.

This move by Japan played right into the hands of the Viet Minh. Their guerrillas began to widen the scope of their attacks. They took, held, and administered several villages and towns north and west of the Red River delta. As their influence spread in northern and central Vietnam, Viet Minh agents also stepped up their agitation in the south, where they were not as strong. The Japanese were hardly pleased by the rise of the Viet Minh. They tried to smash it but failed. All the shaky new regime of Bao Dai could do was stand by helplessly.

As the Japanese position worsened, the Viet Minh readied itself. Its forces moved closer to Hanoi, the northern capital, and maintained a watchful vigil. A National Liberation Committee was set up, with Ho Chi Minh as president. On August 10, after the Japanese offer of surrender to the United States, Ho summoned the people to a general uprising. "The hour has struck for an offensive on all fronts," he said. In the north, on August 17, Giap and his troops entered Hanoi. Soon all public buildings were in their hands. The Bao Dai government merely looked on as these momentous events unfolded. Tran Trong Kim resigned as premier and the emperor asked the Viet Minh to form a new government. Then Bao Dai abdicated. He did not vanish from the scene at once, however. Ho gave him a job as supreme counsellor with his provisional government. On August 25, the Viet Minh in Saigon, in alliance with other groups, also took over the government of Cochinchina. Only ten days had passed since the Japanese surrender and already the Viet Minh were in control of the country.

Ho Chi Minh became president of the new government. Vietnam was declared an independent country and a "democratic republic." President Ho knew that he had little time to consolidate his regime. He had to act fast if he were to prevent the victorious Allies from undoing all he had accomplished so far. Vietnamese independence had been announced on September 2. On September 23, British forces entered South Vietnam and began to disarm the Japanese army. The Allies had divided Vietnam into two separate zones of occupation. British troops controlled the area south of the 16th parallel; Chiang Kai-shek's Chinese forces took over the area north of it.

General Douglas Gracey, commander of the British forces, soon showed where his sympathies lay. His aim, which he did not try to hide, was to restore the French to power in Indochina. Nine days after the British had landed, French troops disembarked from English warships. General Gracey declared martial law in Saigon. Vietnamese could not hold public meetings or publish newspapers. The British also armed French soldiers whose weapons had been taken away by the Japanese.

There was no secret about French intentions. They wanted their empire back. With British approval, French soldiers occupied all public buildings in Saigon. This action was taken so swiftly that it caught the Viet Minh by surprise. Little resistance was offered. Viet Minh flags were removed, and soon the French tri-color flew in their places.

Two days later the Viet Minh struck back. Under the command of Tran Van Giau, communist leader of the Viet Minh "Committee of the South," a counterattack was launched. Savage street fighting broke out in Saigon. Many French and Vietnamese civilians were beaten and killed. To quell this violence, the British used all the means at their disposal. Indian troops attached to the British forces were thrown into the fray. General Gracey also made use of Japanese soldiers whom he rearmed for the occasion.

By early October large French forces were in Indochina, commanded by General Philippe Leclerc. Under Leclerc, the campaign of reconquest began. He was given all possible help by the British, including the use of British troops when they were needed. In four weeks the main strategic areas of the south—Cochinchina—were back in French hands. Driven into the countryside, the Viet Minh began guerrilla tactics. A new High Commissioner for Indochina was appointed by the French. This man, Admiral d'Argenlieu, was a colonialist to the core. His diehard attitudes left little room for negotiation or compromise.

In the north things were different. There the French got no help or sympathy from the Chinese. All Frenchmen venturing into the Chinese-controlled zone had their weapons taken away. This gave Ho a temporary reprieve, but he didn't know how long it would last. So he tried his favorite political maneuver—broadening the base of his support among the people. The Communist party was dissolved. Ho even allowed an election to be held and gave more high posts in his government to nationalists. At the same time, the Viet Minh carried on an underground campaign of murder and reprisal against those Vietnamese who were marked as enemies of the regime.

Ho's fears proved fully justified when the Chinese and the French signed an agreement on February 28, 1946. After secret negotiations, the two powers had struck a bargain. The Chinese agreed to withdraw their troops from Vietnam, leaving the way open for the French to come back. In return, the French gave up all their territory and rights in China. Caught in the middle of this Chinese-French squeeze, Ho could do nothing but make the best of a bad situation. He began his own negotiations with the French. These talks led to a temporary arrangement called a "preliminary convention," which both parties agreed to on March 6. Under its terms, the French could station a limited number of troops in Haiphong, Hanoi, and a few other areas. The Viet Minh regime, on the other hand, was given official recognition as a "free state." Two weeks later, the first French soldiers and tanks entered Hanoi.

Then Ho and Pham Van Dong went off to France for further conferences. Ho was after a permanent settlement, but the French would not give him the complete independence he wanted. Every French offer had so many strings attached to it that the Vietnamese could not possibly accept it. As the talks dragged on, it became clear that nothing lasting would come of them. To Ho, this was a disappointment. The unsettled situation could not be allowed to drift much longer. Ultimately, if no permanent agreement was signed, there was bound to be a clash. There were troubling signs already back in Vietnam, where things were heading for a showdown. In Saigon, Admiral d' Argenlieu had pulled off something of a coup. Without consulting anyone, he had announced the creation of a separate republic of Cochinchina. A puppet regime was set up with a man named Nguyen Van Trinh as premier. Months later, when Dr. Trinh realized that he had been used as a tool by the French, he committed suicide.

The Viet Minh were trying everything they could to win over more sections of the people. Their latest effort was a new national front called the Lien Viet. It included all groups and parties willing to support the government. In spite of its new name, it was the same old Viet Minh with more members, and it was the old name by which it continued to be known. Guerrilla actions grew more frequent in the north. They had never stopped in the south where guerrillas had been fighting ever since the French came back in September, 1945. In the mountains of the north, Vo Nguyen Giap reopened old combat training camps and readied his men for war.

Negotiations between Ho and the French had ended in a deadlock. Finally, Ho left France and returned to Vietnam. Nothing had really been settled. The only thing agreed upon was another conference to be held in January, 1947. The conference never took place. On November 20, 1946, fighting erupted in Haiphong between French and Viet Minh soldiers. The French demanded that the Viet Minh give up the parts of Haiphong they held. When the Viet Minh stayed where they were, French ships in the harbor opened fire and shelled the Vietnamese quarter of the city. Thousands of civilians were killed during the bombardment; according to the French "no more than six thousand." Other estimates ranged as high as twenty thousand.

After the Haiphong massacre, the French made further military demands. Ho stalled for time, leading the French to believe that he would give in. But the wily Viet Minh leader, still looking for a peaceful way out, sent a telegram to the new premier of France, Leon Blum, whom he had known in the old socialist days in Paris. Ho hoped that this personal appeal might avert war. He never had a chance to find out. The message lay around for days in the censor's office in Saigon before it was sent to Paris. By the time the message reached Blum, it was already too late. Faced with a choice of capitulating or fighting, the Viet Minh decided to fight. On December 19, Giap's new army attacked French troops in Hanoi and the Indochina war had begun. The next day Ho Chi Minh summoned the people to battle. Vietnam, he said, would fight on for ten years if it had to.

The Viet Minh retreated from Hanoi after a hard battle. Ho Chi Minh went with them. Army and government melted back into the safety of the mountainous north. There Ho and his staff settled down to the arduous business of fighting a war against a large European power. They were up against seasoned troops armed with modern weapons. Giap's men had not been trained to wage conventional war. They would be limited to what they could do best—hit-and-run guerrilla tactics in the mountains, jungles and deltas; the cities would be left alone, except for the occasional use of terror and assassination.

Three years of bitter but inconclusive fighting followed. French arms were superior, but they could not defeat Giap's elusive legions. Neither could the Viet Minh guerrillas beat the French. Hostilities simply dragged along.

On the political front, Ho kept playing down communism and played up nationalism. To counter this, the French set up their own Vietnamese government around Bao Dai, who had long ago been fired by Ho as his supreme counsellor. The emperor went along with the French, who won him over by promising eventual independence for his country. The results, on the whole, were a disappointment to both Bao Dai and the French. Few leading nationalists joined the government. Ngo Dinh Diem, known for his competence and honesty, refused to serve as premier when the French would not even grant Vietnam the same kind of dominion status that India enjoyed under the British. Though Bao Dai's regime, officially termed the Associate State of Vietnam, did gain recognition from many outside governments, including the United States, it was generally regarded, and perhaps rightly so, as a French puppet.

The war, in stalemate, ground on. The Viet Minh controlled most of the country's territory, while the French held on to the cities and a few urban centers. Economic life was almost at a standstill. Rice exports, for instance, were one-tenth of what they would have been normally. Travel on the roads and railways was hazardous and infrequent. Guerrillas seemed to lurk everywhere. In the countryside the most innocent-looking bush might be hiding a Viet Minh killer. The French dotted the landscape with watchtowers in an effort to provide some protection for travelers, but these often became death traps for their occupants.

Giap's men had proved that they could hold the French to a military draw, but final victory was still a long way off. Something dramatic would have to happen to alter the balance of power. Otherwise, the best that Ho could look forward to was that the French would tire of the game and leave. This didn't seem likely at the moment, even though French losses of men and money in three years of combat had been heavy and public opinion back home was beginning to turn against "the dirty war," as it was called.

The French had no real policy for ending the struggle. Mired down in a political and military impasse, they refused to take the one step that might have brought results —to give Vietnam its independence within the framework of the French Union. But they feared, and they may have been right, that this would encourage their other colonial possessions to break away. So they did nothing, except when they were absolutely forced to by the pressure of events.

The turning point in the Indochina war came at the end of 1949. This occurred, strangely enough, not as a result of anything that happened inside Vietnam. Ever since the end of World War II, the Chinese communists and the Kuomintang armies had been fighting for control of China. Now, Mao and his reds had won. Chiang Kai-shek and the remnants of his nationalist armies left the mainland and retreated to the island of Formosa, leaving Mao master of the most populous nation on earth. What this meant for Asia and the rest of the world only time would reveal. It had, however, an immediate effect on the war in Indochina. For the first time Ho and his fellow revolutionaries had an ally on their borders, from whom they could get help and expert advice. Both were quick in coming. The triumph of the Chinese communists shook up the whole balance of power in Asia. It also turned the tide of battle in Vietnam in favor of the Viet Minh.

Mao's victory in China, coupled with the sagging of French fortunes in Indochina, alarmed the Americans. To show how seriously it now viewed the war between France and the Viet Minh, the United States government announced that it was furnishing the French with economic and military aid. The sputtering French economy was simply no longer able by itself to sustain the burden of the Asian war. American economic and military missions went to Saigon to establish closer liaison with the French and to study events on the spot. Following the outbreak of the Korean War in June, 1950, American anxiety about Southeast Asia increased, and so, too, did the amount of its aid to the French.

The French in Indochina tried to gain political advantage from the altered situation. Overnight, their propaganda line changed. Now they began to call their struggle with the Viet Minh a holy war against the forces of Asian communism, which would engulf the whole continent unless they were halted in time.

The new communist warlord of China, Mao Tse-tung, was willing to help the Viet Minh, but at a price. He didn't like the way Ho was fighting his war and told him how it should be done. He had three main suggestions—political, economic and military. To begin with, it had been a mistake for Ho to disband his Communist party. The party should be reactivated. Also, to secure the support of the peasants, a program of land reform should be carried out in the areas already held by the Viet Minh. As for the military effort, Mao believed that Giap's guerrilla strategy should now be changed to one of mobile warfare.

Ho and the other Viet Minh leaders agreed to try Mao's three-pronged plan. The Indochinese Communist Party was reborn under a new name, the Lao Dong. In the villages, land was divided up among the peasants, while rent and interest rates were reduced. And General Giap began sending the first contingents of his troops into China to be trained in the art of mobile warfare. The Chinese also assigned military advisers to assist Giap in his staff work and field operations.

Until the change in strategy, the Viet Minh had simply

been fighting a war of attrition in the classic guerrilla manner. That kind of war was designed to wear the enemy down slowly. Now, the Viet Minh switched to the Maoist military formula of annihilation. Instead of bleeding the enemy to death, drop by drop, the new strategy aimed to destroy him by a series of shattering blows. This was the method by which Chiang Kai-shek had been defeated in China. The basic idea behind it was beautifully simple. A military target was selected, assaulted by a numerically superior force, and wiped out by the sheer weight of numbers of the attackers. If, for instance, the French were to defend an outpost with fifty men, the Viet Minh would hit it with a full battalion. Soon the French were reeling from a series of minor but heavy defeats.

After these tryouts, Giap was ready for a more ambitious effort. In the fall of 1950, he began an offensive in the north that knocked out, one by one, a whole string of French forts guarding the Chinese border. For the first time since the war's start, the French suffered serious combat casualties that ran into the thousands. This successful campaign by the Viet Minh gave the French pause. Thousands of their best soldiers had been unable to stand off Giap's ragged but revitalized warriors. They had also been driven out of an important northern salient that gave Giap control of the entire border area.

Though the Viet Minh would suffer occasional setbacks, as when they set out to take Hanoi and failed, the pattern of war had entered a new and decisive phase. Giap had gone from the defensive to the offensive. French commanders, however, still believed in victory and dreamed of the day when they would corner Giap's main force and wipe it out. They recalled the crushing Viet Minh defeat near the town of Vinh Yen, when Giap, driving toward Hanoi, had been foolhardy enough to take on French veterans in open field combat. This one time that the communists had stood and fought in conventional style, they had been routed and badly mauled. Ever since, French strategists kept trying to draw Giap into "set-piece" battles, as they called them, but he would not take the bait. Giap had learned his lesson. He would meet the French in head-to-head combat only when it suited his purpose. Meanwhile, his swift mobile tactics of hitting the

91

enemy in force at carefully chosen points kept the French nervous and guessing.

At the end of 1950, the Chinese crossed the Yalu River and went to war in Korea with the United States and the United Nations. For the next few years, while the Chinese fought the American "paper tigers," Giap didn't get as much help from his communist comrades to the north. But he was doing well enough on his own, and there were now few experienced observers in Indochina who thought that the French had even the slimmest chance of winning the war. After the Korean armistice in 1953, when the flow of Chinese war material to the Viet Minh increased again, the odds on the French dropped even lower. Not many believed in a French victory anymore, except some officers who still hoped for the set-piece battle that would miraculously reverse the trend of war. In France, the government and the people grew more disenchanted with the thankless conflict, even though the Americans were now paying most of its staggering costs.

The arrival in 1953 of General Henri Navarre to take command of the French forces gave heart to those who had still not given up. Navarre was supposed to have a master plan that would do what no one had yet been able to do—beat Giap. General Navarre has since denied that there was such a plan, but it was common gossip at the time among his staff members. The plan, in its broad outlines, was to get Giap to fight the kind of engagement he had lost at Vinh Yen in 1950. Others had tried to do this and failed. But Navarre was sure he would succeed.

The French had another reason for wanting a full-scale showdown with Giap. The diplomats had arranged for a conference on the Indochina war to be held in the spring of 1954 at Geneva, Switzerland. France and the Viet Minh had already consented to attend. The United States, Great Britain, Russia and China would also be represented. The French position at Geneva would be stronger if they could come to the conference on the heels of a big victory.

This was the background of events as General Navarre began to bait the trap for General Giap. The trap was actually a fortress that the French built near the town of Dienbienphu in northwestern Vietnam. It was here that Navarre hoped to entice Giap into a major engagement.

The French bet everything they had on this one last gamble.

There were other factors in Navarre's choice of Dienbienphu as the field of battle. The Viet Minh were planning a thrust at Laos, and the fortress was intended to bar their way. The general also had an idea about setting up attack-proof bases throughout Indochina, from which his troops would hunt down guerrillas in what had up to now been enemy-held territory. Dienbienphu was designed to do that, too. But its main purpose was to convince Giap that it was a sitting duck that he could capture and destroy. The French thought Dienbienphu strong enough to withstand any attack the Viet Minh could throw at it. So, too, did American military experts who examined it.

The fortress itself lay in a valley ringed about by hills and jungle. It commanded a few high points, but most of the hills surrounding the French positions would be in possession of the Viet Minh, if and when they came. The military specialists were not particularly worried about this. It would be dangerous only if Giap could place heavy guns there. The French bunkers could stand up under mortar fire, but anything bigger would pound them to bits. The Viet Minh, however, would never be able to lug heavy artillery across the mountains and through the impenetrable jungles leading to Dienbienphu. Not even a military magician like Giap could perform that impossible feat.

For months the French kept parachuting men and supplies into their jungle bastion. Navarre sent in thousands of his best combat veterans, hoping that this would be a further lure for Giap to strike. Would the Viet Minh commander be tempted to tangle with these elite troops in the belief that the exposed stronghold could be breached and taken? Navarre and his officers hoped he would. Each day the French would glance up into the hills to see if the Viet Minh had come yet. Reports had been coming in that told of Viet Minh columns on the march toward the fortress. So the soldiers of Dienbienphu built more dugouts and bunkers as they waited for the onslaught that might or might not come.

During the months of the French buildup, Giap had also been busy. The reports about Viet Minh troop movements had been accurate. Giap was on his way toward Dienbienphu to take up the French challenge. He knew all about the Navarre plan and its theory of the baited trap. He would give General Navarre what he wanted. He would take the bait. He also had a trap of his own to spring.

Giap was in no hurry. The first French parachutists had dropped into Dienbienphu on November 20, 1953. The Viet Minh leader let the French amass their strength there until he was ready. Then his troops began to move in a steady stream toward the heights overlooking the fortress. Thousands of porters marched with the soldiers, carrying the food and supplies that men need to make war. There were also work crews laboring at another task. Slowly, foot by foot, they were hacking their way into the dense jungle and building a road through it. Behind them, pushing, tugging and hauling, came more men with massive artillery pieces that the experts had said could not be transported across such harsh terrain.

Midway in March, 1954, a large Viet Minh army gathered in the hills and looked down at the valley of Dienbienphu. There were the French strong points fully visible on an open plain that ran twelve miles long and four miles wide. The eleven thousand soldiers defending the fortress were woefully outmanned by the forty thousand regulars under Giap's command. The Viet Minh strategist had not forgotten Mao's sage advice—always attack the enemy with overwhelming superior force.

On March 12, Giap's artillery laced the French positions with a thin trickle of fire. This was just a test run for the gunners to get the range. The French were not unduly alarmed by this opening action. They were still unaware of the enormous firepower with which Giap had encircled them. The following day, on the evening of March 13, their grim ordeal began. Where the night had been quiet before, it suddenly exploded into flaming violence as the big guns of the Viet Minh opened up from all sides.

Never had the French in Indochina faced such a barrage. Bunkers collapsed in heaps of rubble. French artillery tried to answer, firing blindly into the hills. The Viet Minh gunners had no such problem. Their targets, precisely pinpointed, were nicely out in the open. One after another the guns of Dienbienphu fell silent as they were destroyed by direct hits.

The blazing inferno of battle lasted fifty-four days. The

French clung stubbornly to each position but their cause was without hope. The human assault waves of Viet Minh infantry could not be stopped. French planes trying to bomb the gun emplacements in the hills could not penetrate the massive antiaircraft fire thrown up by the enemy. Desperate, France asked for an American air strike to relieve the pressure on the fortress and save it from annihilation. President Eisenhower almost said yes to the French request, then decided against it. This was the closest the United States came to entering the war in Indochina.

At battle's end the French had nothing left but their gallantry. The Americans had been their last chance. On May 7, fifty-five days after Giap's artillery started the one-sided contest, the French surrendered. When the guns stopped firing, those who had been fighting for so long looked around in wonder and marveled at the silence. Dienbienphu now belonged to history. It was the worst defeat ever inflicted on a French Colonial army. But France had lost more than a battle here. It had lost the war and its Indochinese empire.

Chapter 7

THE AMERICANS AND THE MANDARIN

O LD eras end and new ones begin. So goes the story of history. World War II had been a watershed in the relations of Europe and Asia. Before it, except for Japan, Europeans dominated the Oriental world. After it, their power there was weakened and destroyed.

As rebellions shook the continent, one by one, the countries of Asia gained their freedom. The European masters left and native ones took their places. The Netherlands' prize possession, the Dutch East Indies, was now the independent state of Indonesia. Britain's days of glory in Asia were also numbered. So far it had lost India, Burma and Singapore, among others. Soon Malaya would follow. Now France, in her twilight of empire, was losing Indochina.

Two superpowers had come out of the war—the United States and Soviet Russia. The nations of Europe took a back seat as these two mammoths contested for world domination. Now a third goliath, Red China, had risen in Asia. Unified again for the first time in centuries, it cast its enormous shadow over lands still boiling over in revolt.

Worried by the situation in Asia, European and American statesmen had called the Geneva Conference to see if they could work out solutions for two current trouble spots—Korea and Indochina. They had just wound up the Korean part of the discussions when the grim news arrived about the fall of Dienbienphu. One day later, on May 8, the delegates began talking about Indochina.

The timing couldn't have been worse for the French. They had hoped to bring a victory to the conference table. Instead, they came bearing the stigma of a painful and humiliating defeat. The Viet Minh had won, and French power had been broken in Asia forever. The issue to be discussed by the diplomats was no longer whether Vietnam should or should not be free. That question had already been decided by war. The matter to be settled now was how to move from war to peace and how to work out the vexing details of independence in terms of power, people and territory.

The American presence at Geneva was a portent of the times. Asia's mounting woes were causing United States policy makers to shift their attention from Europe to the East. Soviet Russia had been the big threat following World War II. But Russian power had been contained and stopped in Europe. The menace of communist expansionism had switched to Asia. Now that Red China was on the scene to mastermind operations and lend its help, the tempo of communist subversion quickened from one end of the continent to the other.

Ho's triumph, in American eyes, was but another sign of the growing strength of China in the Asian theater. Something would have to be done to stop that power from gaining further—but what? There was no force in Asia now to contain the Chinese as there had been in Europe to hold back the Russians. The North Atlantic Treaty Organization—NATO—had been the instrument by which the Americans and their European allies had held the Russian bear at bay in the West. After Geneva, Secretary of State John Foster Dulles would try to create a similar bulwark in Asia—SEATO, or the Southeast Asia Treaty Organization. But this new coalition of states, hastily thrown together by Mr. Dulles, would be much less effective than its European counterpart, even though solidly backed by the United States.

The Americans had originally been opposed to European colonialism in Asia, which they considered outmoded and inhumane. They were surprised and shaken, however, by the growth of communism after the Europeans left. As the power of Europe waned, that of the communists blossomed. Nature, as the saying goes, abhors a vacuum. So does politics. As soon as an empty space appears in the world of political power, something rushes in to fill it. What would fill the power vacuums left by the departing Europeans—nationalism or communism? The West had hoped it would be nationalism. But nationalists in some countries were not making out so well against the communists and, in a few instances, they cooperated with communist parties instead of fighting them.

Even where they opposed the communists, it was no sure thing that they would win. The Chinese nationalists, for instance, under Chiang Kai-shek, had failed to halt Mao's peasant brand of communism. This had been the first major setback for American policy in Asia. Then had come the grinding stalemate of Korea. Now Vietnam, the traditional barrier to Chinese ambitions in Southeast Asia, was in danger of going communist. This, if it happened, would be a complete disaster. Some Americans saw Vietnam as the linchpin that held Southeast Asia together. Remove that pin and the whole structure would collapse. On April 7, while Dienbienphu was still holding out, President Eisenhower had said in a speech, "The loss of Indochina will cause the fall of Southeast Asia like a set of dominoes." This was the origin of the celebrated "domino" theory, in which the loss of Vietnam was seen as the trigger that would set off a chain reaction of communist victories everywhere else. Topple it and the rest of Southeast Asia would topple with it. Vietnam, in a word, was Asia's Berlin. It had to be defended, and with the French leaving, there was only one nation strong enough and willing to take on the onerous task—the United States.

But the Americans could not do the job alone in Vietnam. They needed a stable government there. They also needed a leader they could rely on. He had to be staunchly anti-communist and untainted by past political connections. He also had to be courageous and a good administrator. Vietnamese politicans who met these qualifications could be counted on the fingers of one hand. Many nationalists had either gone over to the Viet Minh or been tarnished by their association with Bao Dai's French-sponsored regime.

There was, however, a nationalist of prominence who had steered clear of both camps. This was Ngo Dinh Diem, the same man who on several previous occasions had turned down the chance to be premier in a Bao Dai government. On June 18, 1954, however, Diem announced that he had accepted a new offer by Bao Dai to head his government. He had set the royal Chief of State stiff conditions. Bao Dai had to agree to give Diem full civil and military powers. This made Diem the real power instead of the emperor.

Several things had happened to make Ngo Dinh Diem change his mind. France, on June 4, had granted the Associate State of Vietnam its independence, so that Diem's government would be completely free of French control. With France on the way out, the coming power in Vietnam was the United States, which had already indicated that it would not stand for a total communist takeover of the country. Under the umbrella of American power, and with its support, Diem stood at least a reasonable chance of surviving a very uncertain and dangerous situation. The Geneva Conference was still going on, and there was no telling what would come out of it. In the meantime, Diem flew back to Saigon from his self-imposed exile abroad and assumed the reins of government. He had waited twenty-one years for this moment.

The personal story of Ngo Dinh Diem, told briefly, has its fascinating aspects. Born in 1901 into a leading Catholic mandarin family, he had a brilliant career as an administrator in the 1920s. Despite his youth, he was picked by the even younger Emperor Bao Dai to be his chief minister at the imperial court. Even then he was known for his honesty and courage. But these traits got him into trouble with the French when he tried to push through some reforms. The French refused, Bao Dai would not back him, and Diem resigned. From that very moment, in 1933, Diem began his trek into the political wilderness that did not end until he became premier in 1954.

Though he was out of office for more than two decades, Diem never doubted that one day he would be called upon to lead his nation. His sense of mission, like that of General de Gaulle of France, was strong. In this he was sustained by a strong religious belief and by his closely knit family. Twice, Diem had refused to become Bao Dai's premier because the conditions were not to his liking. He would take power only on his own terms, and did, finally, when they were met.

One of the stories most often told about him dates back to 1945. After the Japanese surrender, Diem was picked up and arrested by the Viet Minh. Ho Chi Minh heard that Diem was in custody and asked that he be brought to him. When Diem came, Ho offered him a position in his new government. Ho needed good administrators and Diem, he knew, qualified admirably. He was also aware that Diem, as a leading Catholic layman, carried a lot of weight with his co-religionists. Ho wished, through Diem, to gain Catholic support for his government.

Diem turned Ho down at once. His reason for doing so is interesting, for it gives an insight into Diem's personality and his fierce attachment to his family. Instead of saying no to Ho because he was a communist and a political foe, Diem spurned his invitation on purely personal grounds. News of the death of his older brother, Ngo Dinh Khoi, who had been seized and murdered by the Viet Minh, had just recently reached Diem.

"Why," said Diem to Ho, "did you kill my brother?"

Ho tried to explain. "It was a mistake," he said. "The country was all confused. It could not be helped."

Diem did not say another word. He turned and left the room. It was the last time the two men ever met face to face. Later, when Diem was released from jail, he kept out of sight until the French had regained control of some areas of the country.

There is no doubt that without American help, Diem would never have made it as premier. He had impressed influential Americans in Japan in 1950, and then in the United States, where he had lived from 1951 to 1953. This helped his cause when the moment of decision came. During his stay in the United States, Diem lived at the Maryknoll Seminaries in New York and New Jersey. He lectured at universities, went on speaking tours, and made frequent trips to Washington, D.C., where he tried to win the support of important people. One of his strongest champions was New York's Francis Cardinal Spellman. He also became friendly with Justice William O. Douglas of the Supreme Court, Senator Mike Mansfield of Montana, and a rising young Senator named John F. Kennedy.

These contacts were helpful later on, especially when Diem needed a kind word in his behalf.

Diem had always been a lone wolf in politics. He never had a real political party of his own or a large personal following. Most people in South Vietnam had only a hazy notion of who he was when he took office. Only the people at the top knew his merits and abilities. They were also aware of his limitations. Diem was a proud, stubborn man who was bent on having his own way, no matter what. He trusted few, except for his family and some friends. At first these traits would be a source of great strength for him. Later they would prove his undoing.

This was the man the American government backed in the crucial summer of 1954. The French went along with his selection, but not with any real enthusiasm. Diem was too independent to suit them. They still had vast economic interests to protect in Vietnam and they weren't sure that Diem would be cooperative or understanding in these matters. So they hoped he would fail and that another, more acceptable leader would take his place.

Diem took office in Saigon on July 7. The Geneva Conference was still two weeks away from a final agreement. Negotiations were about to be completed after several months of argument and debate. The lengthy sessions, in which much hard bargaining took place, had revealed that a unified Vietnam under a single government was impossible at this moment of history. The United States would never accept communist domination of the entire country, and the Viet Minh would never agree to a national government in which they did not have the leading part. Partition of the country into two distinct halves seemed the only practical solution. Reunification would be postponed to some later date, the details to be worked out by the conference.

The United States played a minor role in these discussions. Secretary of State Dulles had decided against official American participation at the meetings on Indochina. He knew that the Viet Minh could not be prevented from winning a diplomatic victory at the conference; only the size of that victory was still in doubt. Dulles did not want to be party to an agreement that would represent a communist triumph in the eyes of the American people and the Congress. So the secretary left Geneva and went home. An American delegation remained behind and sat in on the proceedings as an "observer."

Both the Viet Minh and the Bao Dai government had originally been opposed to partition. Both had declared themsleves in favor of a unified Vietnam whose government would be chosen by nationwide elections. But the great powers, including Russia and China, took an opposite view. Under great pressure from the Russians and the Chinese, who feared American military intervention if all of Vietnam went to Ho, the Viet Minh dropped their demand for unity and agreed to go along with the partition scheme.

The other Vietnamese regime, which was now headed by Ngo Dinh Diem, held steadfast to the principle of a unified country and registered its firm objection to partition. Its objections, however, were overridden. The main issue to be resolved now was the actual line of demarcation between north and south.

The conference then became, as one writer called it, "a battle of the parallels." The Viet Minh would not settle for anything less than the division of the country at the 16th parallel. The French were equally adamant in their refusal to draw the dividing line there. After much wrangling, climaxed by the intercession of Soviet Foreign Minister Molotov, both sides finally agreed on a demarcation line: the 17th parallel. On July 21, the last day of the conference, representatives of France and the Viet Minh signed an agreement for a military cease-fire, which, in effect, split the country into separate political spheres.

Ho Chi Minh and his Viet Minh would rule the government in the north—the Democratic Republic of Vietnam. The territory south of the 17th parallel, the new state of South Vietnam, would be the domain of Ngo Dinh Diem and Bao Dai. The conference made it clear, however, in its Final Declaration, that the division was not meant to be permanent. It called for elections in two years, during July, 1956, whose purpose would be the reunification of the country under one government.

The United States, which had remained aloof throughout the proceedings, refused to approve the Final Declaration, thus disassociating itself from its conclusions and recommendations. The foreign minister of South Vietnam, Dr. Tran Van Do, also expressed strong opposition to the terms of the French-Viet Minh cease-fire and to the Final Declaration. The conference then adjourned and the delegates went home, not at all certain if what they had achieved in this ancient Swiss city would stand up under the test of future events.

In the north, Ho Chi Minh set about creating a communist state that modeled itself after the Chinese. French forces withdrew in planned stages, and Hanoi, turned over to the Viet Minh, became the capital and seat of its government. In the south, Ngo Dinh Diem found himself in possession of a government that had very little authority outside the city limits of Saigon; and even there its authority was being contested. The country was in a complete state of collapse and chaos. Bandits roamed the rural areas. It was next to impossible to get from one place to another by road or railway. The Viet Minh had pulled up tracks, destroyed trains, and made many roads impassable. They had even, in some places, put barriers in the rivers.

One of the early difficulties involved the great and incessant movement of people from south to north and from north to south. There were fifty thousand Viet Minh troops in the south who had to be repatriated to the north, in addition to another twenty thousand Vietnamese who preferred to live under the Viet Minh. Not all the Viet Minh went north, however. Many of them stayed behind, under orders to lie low for the time being. Arms caches were also buried against the day when they might be needed.

The flow of refugees from the north, 85 per cent of them Catholic, developed into something of a stampede. Nobody on either side had been prepared for such a massive migration of people. Ultimately, 900,000 completed the trek to the south under the most arduous of conditions. The flight of so many people stunned the communists, who hadn't expected it. Northern authorities began to make it more difficult for those who wanted to leave. It is estimated that at least 400,000 more people might have gone south if the communists hadn't stopped them. The plight of those who made it to South Vietnam was pathetic. Eventually, Diem helped them start their own farming and fishing villages. It was one of the more solid achievements of his regime.

Political opposition to the Diem government formed almost at once. It came from three main sources: the army, a criminal syndicate called the Binh Xuyen, and two religious sects, the Cao Dai and the Hoa Hao. The communists during this period were not Diem's main problem. They expected to win the country peacefully when reunification elections were held in 1956, so they remained fairly quiet.

Diem could not deal with his enemies all at once. His strategy was to cope with them one at a time. First, he faced an internal attack by his army chief of staff, General Nguyen Van Hinh. The army, for the most part, wavered in its support of Diem, and Hinh was the strong man of the anti-Diem faction. However, the Americans came to the new premier's aid. General J. Lawton Collins, President Eisenhower's personal envoy to the South Vietnamese government, warned Hinh and his co-conspirators that all American aid would cease if Diem were deposed by force. Two days after Collins laid down the law, Hinh flew off to Europe as an exile and the army threat was over.

The Hinh affair was minor, though, compared to the menace presented by the Binh Xuyen and by the religious sects. The Binh Xuyen were a gang of former river bandits who ran all gambling and vice in Cholon, the Chinese city next to Saigon. To safeguard these and other commercial enterprises, which included a monopoly of the opium trade, they had bought outright control of the Saigon-Cholon police force from Bao Dai, it was reputed, for 40 million piasters! The leader of this crime empire was a swashbuckling cutthroat named Bay Vien, who also had at his disposal a private army of 2,500 men.

The Binh Xuyen, who had mixed crime with politics in their drive for wealth and power, had a colorful and bloody history. Pirates originally, they had built up a racket of extracting tribute from commercial vessels using the Saigon River. In politics, they switched sides as often as it suited them. During World War II, they had worked closely with the Japanese. Then they had swung their support over to the Viet Minh and fought the French during the first years of the Indochina war. But Bay Vien, then a deputy commander with the Viet Minh, broke with Ho and brought his men over to Bao Dai's new Vietnamese army, which had been formed by the French. His help was considered so important that he was made a full colonel—the first Vietnamese to hold this rank. Bao Dai showed his gratitude—and his greed—by selling his criminal allies the right to run the police force.

In Cholon, where the Binh Xuyen had their headquarters, Bay Vien lived like a feudal prince. A moat in front of his house was filled with live crocodiles. When he slept at night, a chained leopard stood sentry at his door. Some of his other quaint pets were a python and a caged tigress, which, according to rumor, dined occasionally on human flesh.

The Cao Dai and the Hoa Hao were another matter entirely. Both—which still exist—are a curious blend of religion and politics, and both came originally out of orthodox Buddhism. Older of the two is the Cao Dai. Its founder, Ngo Van Chieu, was a province chief under the French who had a reputation as a detective and crime expert. Tired of tracking down criminals, he turned to religion and mysticism. He claimed, for one thing, to be in direct contact with the spirit of the famous French writer, Victor Hugo, and had reams of poetry which he said Hugo's ghost had recited to him during their talks. The ex-detective's fame as a prophet grew and he soon had many followers. Cao Daism, which dates from 1919, combines strains of Confucianism, Taoism, spiritualism, and even Catholicism with its basic Buddhism. Heading the sect is a pope. Cao Dai services are held in candy-colored pink and green temples, where its believers worship before the image of an enormous eye, the sect's sacred symbol. In 1954, it had more than two million members and an army of twenty thousand, a formidable force for Diem to contend with.

Tha Hoa Hao, younger of the two sects, came into existence just before the war in 1939. Strange, indeed, were the circumstances of its birth. A peasant's son, Huynh Phu So, suffered from a nervous affliction. One day, as he lay ill during a great storm, he rose from his bed mysteriously cured. This experience changed the young man's life. He became a faith healer who traveled the country spreading the gospel of a new religion, Hoa Hao, which he had named after his native village. The followers who rallied to his banner wore their hair to their shoulders as did the master, and their numbers increased rapidly. Huynh Phu So was murdered by the Viet Minh in 1947, but his order endured. When Diem became premier, the Hoa Hao were a million and a half strong, with an army of fifteen thousand.

The sects came into prominence during the war with the French. Aside from the Viet Minh, they were the only organizations in the country that enjoyed mass popular support. All three groups—the Binh Xuyen, Cao Dai and Hoa Hao—had built up separate power bases in Vietnam. In their respective areas, they operated, more or less, as states within states, levying taxes and running the local administrations. The Cao Dai was concentrated in the section northwest of Saigon, the Hoa Hao in several provinces southwest of the city.

Saigon, when Diem took over, was ridden with crime and corruption. The new premier was determined to clean it up. This meant breaking up the Binh Xuyen. Diem cleverly gave positions in his cabinet to the Cao Dai and Hoa Hao, thus protecting his flanks while he dealt with the nefarious Bay Vien. Diem made further progress when several sect military commanders and their troops came over to the government side.

Early in 1955, Diem was ready to act. Striking swiftly, his troops moved in on the Binh Xuyen gambling dens in Saigon and shut them down. The loss of revenue from these lucrative sources was a severe jolt to Bay Vien and his business associates. At the end of March, Diem decided that the time had come to take military measures against them. Fighting broke out in the streets of Saigon between Binh Xuyen mercenaries and government soldiers. In provoking this battle, Diem acted against the advice of the Americans. The French arranged a temporary truce, but in April hostilities flamed anew. General Collins, more and more irked by Diem's stubbornness, made a special trip to Washington and informed President Eisenhower that Diem had to go. The President agreed to follow Collins' recommendation. Then came the word from Saigon that Diem, whose palace had been besieged by the Binh Xuyen, had turned the tables on his opponents and was winning. Immediately, the American policy changed back again to firm support of Diem and all ideas about getting rid of him were dropped.

Pushed out of Saigon, the Binh Xuyen fled to the swamp country that lay east of the city. There they were surrounded and their retreat cut off. Diem waited until September before launching an offensive that wiped out the last enemy remnants. With the Binh Xuyen crushed, only the Hoa Hao and Cao Dai remained to be taken care of. Diem used a combination of military, political and economic means to accomplish this. While the Hoa Hao armies were being attacked and routed in their Mekong Delta sanctuary, Diem was buying off their top leaders with bribes and jobs in the government and army. Only the sect's chief, the colorful and implacable Ba Cut, refused to give up the struggle. He fought on until April, 1956, when he was captured and executed.

Northwest of Saigon, the Cao Dai forces, seeing the handwriting on the wall, had been coming over to the government side in droves. Most of those who were left allowed themselves to be taken peacefully and disarmed. A few leaders held out, among them Phan Cong Tac, the Cao Dai pope, who crossed over into neighboring Cambodia and carried on his fight from there. But it was only a shadow opposition without great threat or meaning. In a little more than a year, Ngo Dinh Diem, who nobody thought would last, had triumphed over all his opponents. Now only one man barred his path to total power—the emperor himself, Bao Dai.

Diem took care of this last obstacle easily enough. An election was held in October, 1955, in which the two principal opponents were Premier Diem and Chief of State Bao Dai. The final vote was overwhelmingly in Diem's favor. Out of almost six million ballots cast, Diem received 5,722,000 votes, while the emperor's total was a mere 63,000. In ousting Bao Dai, the people also approved the end of the monarchy and the establishment of a republic, with Diem as president.

The enormous margin of victory led many to suspect that the vote had been rigged by Diem's brother, Ngo Dinh Nhu, who had organized the election. Those who knew the cunning Nhu believed him to be capable of practically anything. He liked subterfuge and intrigue, and anything involving a plot. Nevertheless, this was the relative Diem felt closest to and came to depend on more and more. Brother Nhu, an ex-librarian by profession, had political ambitions of his own. Diem's rise to eminence gave him the opportunity that he had long been waiting for, and he set about creating a political organization that would be loyal to him.

The Personalist Labor Revolutionary Party, or Can Lao, as it was known, was founded by Nhu in 1956. Never really a party in the true sense of that word, it was used mainly as an espionage agency for Nhu and his brother, the president. Can Lao members and agents were placed in key spots in the government, administration and army. Anyone suspected of being a communist or an enemy of the regime was reported to Nhu. Thus, he was able to keep his finger on the pulse of the country, for Can Lao spies might be found anywhere from a school to a factory to a local village. No one ever knew how many members Nhu's party had, for its lists were secret. Guesses ranged widely between five thousand and fifty thousand. Diem's brother had modeled the Can Lao after another totalitarian organization he admired—the communist party. Nhu never denied this. It did not seem to bother him that he was using communist methods to fight communism. Nor was he at all perturbed that the Can Lao was also being used to browbeat and persecute other political groups and parties.

Now that Diem had won out over all his foes, the brothers wished to make sure that no one else would unseat them. On the surface, South Vietnam was a republic with a brand-new constitution promising freedom and democracy to its people. In practice, however, the very opposite was true. President Diem, who believed in a single, strong executive, concentrated all power in his own hands. He had made certain of this by eliminating the office of premier, so that there was no one to rival him at the top. Although the constitution called for a popularly elected National Assembly and a free court system, both the legislature and the courts were, in actuality, held tightly in line by the president. Nhu was Diem's right arm in all these matters. He fixed elections, packed the National Assembly with his henchmen and hirelings, and sent his Can Lao prowling the country in search of dissenters.

Gradually, under the cloak of constitutional government, a personal and family dictatorship was being born. The Ngo Dinh family was a remarkable one, indeed. In addition to brother Nhu, there was his wife, Madame Nhu, a beautiful, brave and power-hungry woman. Then there were three other brothers, each of whom helped Diem in different ways. Monsignor Ngo Dinh Thuc, a prelate of the Catholic Church, gave the president spiritual advice and also advised him about more practical matters. Ngo Dinh Can, in many ways the strangest of the brothers, ran Central Vietnam for Diem and ruled it like a medieval prince. This strict, severe man wore traditional mandarin clothes and slept on a bare floor, as his ancestors had done. Few liberties were allowed in Can's domain, even less than in Saigon. Another brother, Ngo Dinh Luyen, served as a diplomat abroad. Luyen had tried to get Diem to pursue a more liberal policy, but Nhu was against it. When Nhu won out over Luyen as Diem's chief adviser, the die was cast and the march toward dictatorship began.

The Americans did not particularly like what Diem and Nhu were up to, but neither were they very critical of them. Conditions in the country were still so precarious that nobody wanted to rock the boat by protesting too loudly. The miracle of Diem's survival, after all the dire predictions of his downfall, was still fresh in everyone's mind. Victory over the sects and Bao Dai had given him a stature he never had before. American officials hoped that he would now make his regime more democratic by allowing political opposition; but they failed to insist when he didn't. So long as Diem fought the communists and cooperated in military matters, they would go along, too.

To the Americans, at the time, the danger from the outside seemed more important than anything that was happening on the inside. As the summer of 1956 approached, it appeared that the two Vietnams, North and South, were moving on a collision course that could end in war. In August, 1955, Diem had informed North Vietnam that he would not hold the national reunification elections called for by the Geneva Conference and set for July, 1956. He did not feel bound by agreements that he had neither signed nor approved. Diem also stated that free elections in a communist state were impossible and he would never be party to a fake referendum that sold the Vietnamese people into slavery.

The communists reacted angrily to Diem's announcement. They had hoped to win all of Vietnam through these elections and Diem had slammed the door in their faces. With this avenue cut off to them, they could now only take the country by force. The big American worry was that Ho's armies would come sweeping down into the south just as the North Korean communists had invaded South Korea in 1950. That was why they were training South Vietnam's army to repel an assault in strength across the 17th parallel. The pick of Diem's officer corps was being sent off to the United States and Okinawa for instruction in the art of conventional warfare. Many critics pointed out that this was the wrong kind of training for the type of war that would probably be fought in South Vietnam—a guerrilla war. These critics were, of course, right. That was exactly the kind of war the communists would fight when they decided the time was ripe.

The Viet Minh cadres left behind by Ho had already formed an underground apparatus in South Vietnam. Diem had complained about such illegal activity when he turned down the north's demands for elections. To counteract Viet Minh influence, Diem initiated a program aimed at restoring his regime's authority in the villages. It proved to be a difficult job, which worked better in some areas than in others. Where the Viet Minh was strong, the program could make little headway. Nevertheless, Diem tried. His soldiers went in first to establish government control. They were followed by civilian teams which had been specially trained by the Americans to deal with village and rural problems.

Dressed in peasant garb—black pajama trousers and blouses—the teams made friends with the people and explained that they were there to help them. When they proved it, by building medical dispensaries, roads and schools for their children, the peasants began to trust them. Many peasants volunteered to serve in the Self Defense Corps units that were organized in their villages to protect them from outside attack. Recruits were given weapons and taught how to use them. Peasants also joined a new regional force called the Civil Guard, whose job it was to man defense posts at strategic points in the countryside.

These early successes heartened Diem, who believed that an armed people at the grass roots level was the best bulwark against communism. But the fragile bond between the president and the peasant did not last long. Diem himself

110

and his brother Nhu were responsible for severing it. The sinister operations of the Can Lao produced feelings of hatred and hostility toward the Ngo Dinh brothers. Early in 1956, Diem issued an ordinance making it possible to send to a concentration camp those who were deemed to be "a danger to the state." Under this broad definition, the government was able to arrest anyone it pleased. Not only communists, but democrats and liberals as well, fell victim to this decree. It was, as a matter of fact, Diem's noncommunist opponents who were hit hardest by it.

Then, in the summer of 1956, came what many considered to be the president's greatest blunder. Village mayors and councils had always, by tradition, been elected. Diem abolished this age-old practice and ruled that henceforth the officials would be appointed by his provincial chiefs. He took this drastic step to keep the Viet Minh from being elected to positions of power in the villages. It did that, all right, but it also added to the regime's growing reputation for oppression and tyranny. The only ones who benefited from the move were those it was meant to hurt —the Viet Minh. They pointed to it as but the latest of Diem's dictatorial measures, which it was.

Villagers looked upon the government with growing suspicion and distrust. Communists fed on these dissatisfactions. They attacked Diem as a dictator and called him a traitor to Vietnam and an American puppet because he stood in the way of elections that would have reunified the country. This propaganda was very effective.

Midway in 1957, Diem decided to move against the Viet Minh. He chose what he thought was the right time to do it. Feeling in the south was running strong against the communists. There had been reports from North Vietnam about communist brutalities committed against the people. Ho's government had tried to force a policy of land reform on the unwilling peasants. Many had risen in revolt and fought back. More than 100,000 perished and 500,000 more were arrested. Finally, Ho called a halt to the terror. But his personal reputation as a moderate revolutionary and patriot had suffered serious damage.

Feeling that he had public opinion on his side, Diem launched his raids on the Viet Minh strongholds. So long as Ho's followers were at large, communism had a base in the south from which it could strike. By acting to crush

111

them, Diem intended to put an end to this internal threat. He sent his police into the countryside to arrest hundreds of the "Viet Cong," as he contemptuously called them. The term itself means "Vietnamese communist," but as used loosely by Diem it often took in practically anyone else who opposed him. While his men rounded up the real Viet Cong, they also seized other oppositionists, among whom were democrats, liberals, socialists and sect members. Those who fell into the police net were shipped off to concentration camps, which the government, with a straight face, called "political re-education centers."

Many of the hunted joined forces with the Viet Cong, who were beginning to move from talk and leaflets to armed action. Terrorist bands, which had never been completely inactive, became bolder and more daring. Government officials were murdered and kidnaped. Villagers were warned not to cooperate with Diem's representatives on pain of reprisal. Slowly, the rebel campaign in the rural districts spread. The Americans and the Vietnamese army had based their military strategy on a communist invasion from the north. This strategy would soon have to be revamped. What was brewing in South Vietnam was something far more threatening—a full-scale guerrilla war that would try to capture the country from within.

Chapter 8

GUERRILLA WAR AND THE VIET CONG

ONE of the things Americans found out about the war in Vietnam, as it grew, was that it was unlike any war they had ever been in before. If it had been a guerrilla war and nothing else, it would not have been nearly so dangerous. For guerrilla warfare is simply a style of fighting that has been used by men ever since ancient times. But this war was strange and different. It was a revolutionary war in which guerrilla warfare was only one of the methods of combat. The Viet Cong were aiming at more than just a military victory. Their war, at its heart, was political. What they wanted was total power, so they could change things from top to bottom. And they weren't waiting until the war was over before they made these changes. They were making them now, as they fought. Their goals were threefold. Thus, they were trying to win a war, overthrow a government, and make a social revolution—all at the same time. This was a tall order and might take many years to accomplish. But they had time and they had patience, and they were sure that their enemies had neither.

To have any chance of winning, however, they needed one more element—the people. Without the people on their side they could neither survive nor hope for victory.

It was this factor—the support of the people—that became the key to the war. Whoever won the people would win the war.

American military planners did not grasp this fact until late in the game. When they did, they realized that what the communists were up to in Vietnam went beyond mere warfare. This was an insurrection made up of interlocking parts. The military part was guerrilla warfare—war by stealth, surprise, ambush, raid. The political part was subversion, propaganda, persuasion. Then there was another part—the special terror section whose main purpose was to strike fear in the hearts of the enemy and of anyone else who opposed the rebellion.

There was nothing in the old military books about this new kind of conflict. To call it a guerrilla war, as many did, was not really accurate, as we have seen. So a name was invented that seemed to fit it better, one that took account of its revolutionary and subversive character—"insurgency." The strategy devised to defeat it, "counter-insurgency," combined guerrilla tactics with nonmilitary programs that would win the people away from the insurgents.

The political element in insurgency was new, but the military aspect of it was old. The Viet Cong guerrillas were part of a long tradition. History abounds with examples of guerrilla wars and famous guerrilla chieftains, many of whom have been Americans.

The word itself, however, "guerrilla," is of relatively recent vintage. It comes from *guerra*, the Spanish word for war and means, literally, "small war." There are many early instances of guerrilla warfare, or combat by small groups of armed men against larger, regular armies. Imperial Rome's frontier forces and armies of occupation were constantly harassed by local guerrillas. Other ancient kingdoms and empires were similarly beset. The expression, though, was coined during the Peninsula War (1808-1814), when bands of Spanish patriots fought the invading legions of Napoleon to a standstill. Later, when England's Duke of Wellington whipped Napoleon at Waterloo, he was able to do so more easily because Spanish guerrillas kept a large part of the French forces pinned down in Spain.

Americans learned something about the wily ways of

114

the guerrilla during colonial days. The Indian, whose war-like habits they studied out of necessity, was an expert at forest fighting. The white man living in the wilderness picked up the cunning art of the red man in self-defense. But the European new to the continent was literally a babe in the woods when it came to Indian warfare. This was also true of soldiers who had been trained for open field combat. A case in point is the disaster that befell General Edward Braddock during the French and Indian Wars.

In 1755, as they marched to storm Fort Duquesne near the present site of Pittsburgh, crack British regulars under Braddock were routed by a mixed force of Indian and French guerrillas. These doughty forest warriors, though outnumbered, beat Braddock's men badly, killed Braddock himself, and taught the Britons a lesson in Indian fighting they never forgot. Some of the British escaped only because a young American on the general's staff knew his way around the country and led them out of the ambush. Years later all of England would know his name and wish it didn't—George Washington.

The British, in the same wars, also had their own celebrated guerrilla unit, known as "Rogers' Rangers." Led by Major Robert Rogers, an American, this vaunted six-hundred-man corps knew every trick there was to know about Indian fighting. The French and their Indian allies had good reason to fear Rogers and his buckskin-clad men who had thrashed them in many a backwoods campaign. The dash, courage and exploits of the Rangers spread their fame all the way to Europe.

Another guerrilla leader of great repute was Lieutenant Colonel Francis Marion of South Carolina. Marion made his mark during the American Revolution as a will-o'-the-wisp guerrilla leader whose deeds became legendary. His lightning raids against the Redcoats and his ability to escape afterward to his swamp hideout, where he literally vanished, earned him the nickname of "The Swamp Fox."

During the American Civil War, both sides used guerrillas, but Colonel John S. Mosby of the Confederacy was by far the outstanding guerrilla captain produced by that conflict. Like a gray ghost, he eluded pursuit and capture for years as he spread havoc behind the enemy lines. His troops of mounted guerrillas were always on the move, fighting pitched battles with Union cavalry, cutting communications, and stealing supplies. Mosby staged one of his most spectacular feats when he slipped past the Federal defenses and captured a northern general and thirty-three of his men.

Colonel T. E. Lawrence—the fabulous Lawrence of Arabia—was the first guerrilla commander to win renown in modern times. This pint-sized English archeologist was a member of British Intelligence during World War I. Ordered to make trouble for the enemy Turks in the Middle East, he organized a motley group of Arab warriors into a superb guerrilla fighting machine. Britain's eventual victory over Turkey in that sector of the war was, almost single-handedly, the work of this quiet, shy scholar who had a talent close to genius for waging guerrilla war in the desert sands of Arabia.

The importance of guerrilla war as a way of immobilizing large enemy forces was amply proven during World War II. Thousands of German and Japanese troops were kept so busy chasing Allied guerrillas in Europe and Asia that they couldn't be used for combat duty on the war's critical battle fronts. Many famous guerrilla outfits were formed in lands occupied by the Axis powers—the French Maquis, the Partisans of Yugoslavia and Italy, the American-led forces in the Philippines, and the British in Southeast Asia.

Military men had always thought of guerrillas as a valuable but minor part of warfare. They were helpful for operations of a limited scale, but they were never intended to be used as the main instrument of battle. That task was still reserved for the regular armies. The communists changed all that. Their strategists, after World War II, reversed the whole approach to war. In the manual of warfare, as they rewrote it, guerrillas would form the bulk of the fighting force during the initial stage of conflict. Conventional armies would be withheld from combat—and then released for the final assault. Only after the enemy had been softened up by a protracted period of subversion, political penetration and terror would their regular divisions take the field and move in for the kill. This, again, was the communist recipe for victory that had been cooked up by the master chef of revolutionary war, Mao Tse-tung. It had been tried and tested successfully in China. Now it was available for export.

The French had succumbed to it in Indochina. The British were presently having their hands full trying to put down a communist insurgency in Malaya, and would succeed only after a lengthy struggle of almost thirteen years. Even noncommunists—like the Algerians—used Mao as a guide in their guerrilla uprisings. In Cuba, in 1956, Fidel Castro had the help of Ernesto ("Che") Guevara, a young Marxist firebrand who had studied the military writings of Mao. "Che" later wrote his own book on guerrilla war, as did Vo Nguyen Giap, the victor of Dienbienphu. Revolutionists who aspired to start and lead a guerrilla revolt read the works of the big three—Mao and "Che" and Giap—and learned how.

The basic rule was still Mao's famous dictum that likened the guerrilla to a fish in and out of water. The guerrilla, Mao had written, is to the people as a fish is to water. Take the people away from him and the guerrilla must perish. That is why, when the guerrilla had the peasant, he was invincible, and without him, nothing. Mao had learned about war and revolution in a land where most of the people were peasants. Before the rise of Mao, communist revolutions, based on the Russian model, had started in the cities and then flowed out into the countryside. After Mao, in the backward countries of Asia and Africa, they began on the farms and in the villages. First win the peasant, said Mao. The cities will fall later, after they have been isolated, surrounded and besieged. It is the peasant, therefore, whom the revolutionary guerrilla must woo and conquer. How does he do this?

Let us consider the peasant. What are the things he wants? First, he wants land of his own. Then he wishes to be rid of the landlord and the tax collector, and to live in peace, free of oppression. The guerrilla promises the peasant that he will put an end to exploitation and injustice. When he rules, the peasant will get his land and the landlord will go. He also gives his word that he will govern justly, tax all equally, and give the peasant a voice in his own government. This is something the peasant has never had before, so the prospect has great appeal for him.

Once the guerrilla has the peasant with him, he can act with great confidence. Now he has secure bases from which he cannot be dislodged. In conventional warfare there are formal battle areas, but there are none for the guerrilla. For him, the front is everywhere. It is wherever he goes or decides to strike. His greatest assets are secrecy and mobility. He keeps his movements secret, so the enemy will not know where he is. And he stays on the move, so the enemy will not catch him even if he finds out where he is. Since he fights only when he wishes to, it is he who has the initiative and the other side which must be alert and watchful. In the words of Mao: "Enemy advances, we retreat; enemy halts, we harass; enemy tires, we attack; enemy retreats, we pursue."

The guerrillas of the Viet Cong did as Mao advised. They went to the people. In this they followed in the footsteps of the old Viet Minh, whose successors they were. There was one fundamental difference. In this war they were not fighting for their freedom against the French. This time they were out to upset a sovereign government run by native Vietnamese. They were also, whether they realized it or not, challenging the power of the United States, which was pledged to help South Vietnam keep its independence.

So the war began, almost casually. There were no soldiers and no battles between armies. Raids, murders, kidnapings—these were its trademarks. It is hard to pinpoint this war in time because, unlike conventional conflicts, it had no formal start. Still, it can be said generally that the Viet Cong insurgency, as we know it, dates from 1957, the same year Diem sent his punitive expeditions into the villeges. Its origins, to put it mildly, are murky. Because it was born in the shadows, so to speak, in the deltas, jungles, mountains and swamplands, the facts about its beginnings are hard to come by. Was the rebellion a communist plot from the outset? Or was it a genuine movement of resistance against Diem that was gradually taken over by the communists? The truth, according to Vietnam authority Bernard Fall, lies somewhere in the middle. There was certainly a communist plan to conquer the south, which Ho's party in the north knew about and probably helped draw up. But the task of the Viet Cong would have been much harder if Diem had rallied the people around him instead of turning them against him.

Diem's manhunts made him many enemies. Even his staunchest supporters began to question the wisdom of the course he had chosen. Only the communists stood to gain from his methods of coercion and terror, for they always did their best fishing in troubled waters. What was feared came to pass. The Viet Cong made common cause with Diem's foes. Front groups sprang up with programs and slogans that had wide appeal. To mask their purpose, communist ideas were never mentioned. Such fronts, which gave the outward appearance of broad public participation, were a favorite communist tactic. Ho Chi Minh, you will recall, had also formed nationalist fronts as a cover for his real aims.

The peasants, too, had lost their faith in Diem. They did not like the way his police raided their villages and shamed the people by setting them against each other as spies and informers. Nor did they approve of his land reform program which, in many areas, brought back the landlords and made the farmers pay for land that they had been using rent-free ever since the Indochina war. So when the Viet Cong came and promised to do away with rent and reduce taxes, the people listened. Some villages went over to the insurgents and became bases for them and sources of supply. Even those that did not join them were becoming cautious and afraid. Caught between the government and the Viet Cong, the peasant looked to save his own skin. Diem's police and soldiers, working in the daylight hours when it was safe, found themselves up against a wall of silence and suspicion. Their sources of information were drying up. No longer would the villagers tell them where to find their quarries. Those who did tell were marked for death and executed as a warning to others.

One of the oddest and most puzzling aspects of the Viet Cong insurgency is that it was allowed to develop under the very noses of Diem and the Americans. The communist guerrillas, with little opposition, took over much of the countryside. Terror and persuasion were their weapons. Few in the villages dared stand in their way without outside help. Diem's Civil Guards and Self-Defense Corps were barely able to defend themselves, let alone others. His army and police were not much better, and seemed bewildered by the whole thing.

The number of slain officials mounted in a pattern familiar to revolutionary war experts. But the Americans, oblivious to any danger except that posed by conventional

119

war, were blind to the threat. Viet Cong terrorists were described by them as "bandit remnants" that would fade away as soon as they were curbed by firm police measures. Some critics have said that the United States military in South Vietnam were then suffering from a "Korea" complex. That is, they were so convinced that the war, when it came, would duplicate the one in Korea that they could not imagine fighting any other kind.

The generals were not the only ones who held to this view. Many civilian officials did, too, among them the American ambassador, Elbridge Durbrow. Diem and a few of his generals, who knew something about Maoist warfare, warned that the communists were busy building political bases in the provinces that would later be turned to military use. The Americans, however, were not convinced. To them, the north, with its army of 350,000 men, was still the primary foe. Compared to that ominous threat, the few terrorists in the village were of minor importance. In Washington, the Pentagon, headed by Admiral Arthur Radford, took the same stand and the old strategy prevailed. So the Vietnamese army sat and waited for an invasion that never came, leaving the Viet Cong free to concoct its devil's brew in the countryside without major challenge.

This ostrich-like policy gave the communists a few years headstart in the undercover war they were waging. Even as late as April, 1959, Pentagon spokesmen were assuring the American people that the guerrillas "had ceased to be a menace to the government" and that the South Vietnamese were "now able to maintain internal security." These were the opinions of Major General Samuel L. Myers in his testimony before the Senate Foreign Relations Committee in Washington. General Myers should have been in a position to know, for he was then the deputy to General Williams, commander of MAAG, the United States Military Assistance Advisory Group in South Vietnam.

The senators on the Committee believed what they were told, and the report they issued in February, 1960, gave this optimistic conclusion: ". . . on the basis of the assurance of the Military Aid Mission in Vietnam . . . at least the U.S. Military Aid Advisory Group (MAAG) can be phased out of existence in the foreseeable future." These

120

words were published at the very moment that Viet Cong assassins were killing more than ten government officials each day. This was a sharp rise in the rate from the year before when ninety a month were being slain. The executions on an organized scale had started in 1957, when seven hundred of Diem's appointees were murdered. Since then the figure had increased steadily from year to year. Victims were selected with care. Anyone who worked for the central government was a likely target. School teachers, health and agricultural experts were singled out and given the special Viet Cong treatment. In some cases this amounted to abduction and threats; in others, death.

Murders of village chiefs were carried out in a precise, prearranged way, so that a clear pattern emerged. Only bad officials and good officials were killed. Those who were neither good nor bad—the mediocre—were left alone. The bad were killed to please the villagers who had often been treated harshly and unfairly by them. The good were killed because they showed the Diem regime in its best light. The mediocre were unharmed because they played no role either way.

There was other evidence of a planned conspiracy. Between 1957 and 1959, the government had unearthed more than 3,500 arms caches. The weapons had been greased and wrapped so that they wouldn't rust in their hiding places. These secret arsenals contained a wide range of military hardware—rifles, machine guns, mortars, bazookas, mines and ammunition. There was also a varied assortment of items, such as typewriters and electric generators. But this was only a fraction of the war material that had been buried by the Viet Minh after the partition in 1954. While there was still hope that the Viet Minh could win by ballots instead of bullets, the arms stayed buried. As soon as it became clear that Diem had sealed off this route to victory, the old Viet Minh fighters dug up their guns.

The communist design was plain enough. It was to break the control of the central government in the hamlets and villages and to put their own rule in its place. To do this, they had to cut the ties between the regime and the countryside. They did it by discrediting Diem and by winning the people over to their side. They also made it unpopular—and unhealthy—for anyone to work for the gov-

121

ernment and against them. Diem could not stop this slow erosion of his power and authority. As for his American advisers, they did not even know what was happening, or how serious it was.

Yet there was nothing mysterious about it. A creeping disease of subversion was imperiling the noncommunist half of Vietnam. The statistics of murder and terror, like those on a fever chart, showed that the temperature of the patient—South Vietnam—was slowly going up. In politics, as in medicine, a fever that is not checked will prove fatal. But the Americans did not recognize the symptoms. They judged the Viet Cong by normal military standards. Therefore, the guerrillas could not be winning because they avoided battle and ran away when challenged.

The summer of 1959 saw another stage of the Viet Cong conspiracy unfold, that of open guerrilla warfare. Moving to the offensive, the insurgents began to attack military bases. For the first time, too, soldiers from the north were trickling into the south, and joining the fight. Until this happened, North Vietnam had kept its role hidden in what appeared to be strictly a southern affair. Now, however, it was beginning to show its hand. The Viet Cong had made solid gains in their struggle with Diem, but the northern leaders were still not satisfied with the rate of progress. At some time in 1958—it is not known exactly when—they sent one of their top men, Le Duan, on a secret inspection tour of the south. Le Duan made a thorough study of the Viet Cong military and political structure and concluded that it had to be helped and strengthened if victory was to be won.

After he returned to Hanoi, Le Duan appeared before the Lao Dong central committee and laid out his blueprint for a new course of action. The party chiefs approved Le Duan's plan and set the wheels in motion to carry it out. This revised guide for the southern insurrection made some critical changes. One was the creation of a communist-run front organization—the National Liberation Front —that would direct all future political operations in South Vietnam. The military arm of the NLF, as the front came to be called, was to be a People's Liberation Army that would absorb all the present Viet Cong fighting units under a central command. A decision was also made to widen the scope of guerrilla activities and to bolster the

122

southern forces with contingents of armed men from the north.

The first movements of such troops began in July, 1959. Mostly southerners who had gone north in 1954, they could expect to be warmly welcomed when they returned to their native areas. The infiltrators came by land and sea. Some traveled in junks that sailed down the coastline. Others slipped across the border at the 17th parallel. These were the simplest and most direct routes to the south. They were also the most hazardous. There was a third way to come, starting in Laos, but this meant a journey of months across mountains and through jungles. The most arduous of the three, it was still the safest. Called the "Ho Chi Minh Trail," it became the main source of infiltration into the south. Beginning on a modest scale, with a few hundred in 1959, the influx of men jumped to about three thousand in 1960 and more than ten thousand in 1961.

The men from the north had been trained to assume positions of leadership in the Viet Cong insurgency. They took over top-ranking posts at every point of operations, from the staff level down to the squad. There were also specialists in weapons and communications, and party propagandists who watched over the political education of the troops. Some of the infiltrators became officials in local Viet Cong governments and sat on committees whose assignment was to build the communist machine in the south and make it more powerful.

The one big national front envisioned by Le Duan took time to organize. It was finally unveiled at the end of 1960. On December 20, all the anti-Diem front groups gathered at a congress and voted to form a single organization to which they would all belong—the "National Front for the Liberation of South Vietnam." Its chairman and ostensible leader was Nguyen Huu Tho, a former lawyer with a long record of activity in communist-sponsored causes. One plank of a ten-point program issued by the NLF showed who the real boss was. Point Four pledged "to carry out land rent reduction, guarantee the peasants right to till their present plots of land, and redistribute communal land in preparation for land reform." This was exactly the same scheme, step-by-step, that had been carried out by the communists in the north and that had led to their campaign of extermination and terror from 1954 to 1956.

The Viet Cong armed forces, under the new People's Liberation Army setup, were divided into two separate categories: the full-time soldiers and those who fought only part of the time. The regulars, or "hard core" units, whose only job was soldiering, were composed almost exclusively of troops from the north. Organized along classic military lines, their chain of command reached all the way to Hanoi, where the important decisions were made. The part-time fighters—or guerrillas—were, by comparison, amateurs, though there were many more of them than there were regulars. Most of the guerrillas worked for a living during the day and turned into marauders and killers only when the sun went down.

Political cadres also went into action at night. By now, practically every village in the deltas had a Viet Cong cell, even those they didn't control. Some of these cells had no more than four or five members. But even with small groups like these they were able to keep the villagers in line. Their reputation alone was enough to frighten people into submission. Thus, a mere handful of Viet Cong could dominate an area where hundreds and sometimes thousands of people lived and labored.

When the Viet Cong came into a village, waving flags and chanting slogans, the evening belonged to them. Peasants had to sit and listen quietly to political lectures, even if they didn't understand, as they often didn't. Radios and loudspeakers blared forth propaganda and no one was foolish enough to object. The Viet Cong also used these visits to collect taxes, which they took in either rice or money. Under the new system, a Viet Cong village became part of a network of local "shadow" governments, all deriving their authority from the National Liberation Front.

In three and a half years, the Viet Cong revolt had come a long way. By 1961, the Front could claim that it, and not Diem, was the government in 80 per cent of the countryside, and that its influence was felt and feared in the remaining rural districts. Only the cities remained firmly under government control, but bomb-throwing terrorists kept the urban populations jittery and alert. No longer could the guerrillas be dismissed airily as "bandit remnants," as they had been only a short while before. Not until Ho's infiltrators started arriving in the south—and the military phase of the rebellion began to expand—did the American military commanders in Vietnam finally admit that there was in fact an insurrection in the country. They had tried to save face by pointing to the "invasion" from the north as the source of the trouble, rather than the native rebellion that had been going on for years. But the truth was that they had failed to see the real danger while it took root, grew and spread all around them.

What had started in the rice paddies as a series of skirmishes, murders and kidnapings was now a full-fledged war. The Diem government, by its own efforts, had been unable to stop the rampaging Viet Cong. All that the Americans had done so far was give money, technical help, and advice. Diem accepted the money, but the only advice he took seriously came from brother Nhu and other members of his family.

The dictator President still refused to work with other politicians or parties, even though he needed all the help he could get in his mortal struggle with the communists. So the complaints and criticisms grew louder from those Vietnamese who felt that the greatest obstacle to victory was the rule of the imperious Ngo Dinh family. As matters worsened, the United States found itself confronted with two perplexing problems in Vietnam. One was the Viet Cong insurgency that threatened to engulf the whole country. The other was the proud mandarin they had helped boost to power in South Vietnam—Ngo Dinh Diem.

Chapter 9

THE DECLINE AND FALL OF NGO DINH DIEM

DIEM had never been a popular leader. He was much too remote and aloof for that. Crowds made him uneasy. Like most mandarin aristocrats, he lacked the common touch. Even in face-to-face conversations it was hard for anyone else to get in a word. The President never talked to you. He talked *at* you. Newspapermen and others who went to interview him at his palace for the first time went away with dazed looks on their faces, numb from the experience. It was not unusual for visitors to be kept virtual prisoners by Diem while he delivered tedious non-stop lectures at them lasting for hours. Only rarely did anyone get a chance to talk back or even ask a question. When that happened, the inscrutable head of state merely stared past the offender with expressionless black eyes and went on speaking as if he hadn't heard. American officials went through the same ordeal.

Diem's hold on the people, never great, had slipped badly since 1957, when his power was at its peak. That was also the year when the first attempt was made on his life. The incident occurred while Diem was attending a rural fair outside of Saigon. The would-be killer, who was not caught, took a shot at him and missed. Though Diem came away unscathed, it was a sharp warning that all was not well.

Brother Nhu was well aware that the regime faced difficult days in the years ahead. To hold on, the Ngo Dinh family would have to keep an even tighter rein on things. Such matters were left to Nhu, who ran the secret police as well as the Can Lao. Only a few of those who worked for him had his trust. The rest were watched closely. Security measures even extended into the army. Favoritism became the only method by which officers were given important posts or promoted. If a soldier was known to be loyal to the Ngo Dinh family, he could be sure of advancement. If not, either he stayed where he was or he was demoted. This embittered those who were passed over, especially if they were men of ability. But Diem and Nhu cared nothing about that. The army might be less efficient because of it, but so much the worse for the army—and for the war, if it came to that.

New elections to the National Assembly were held in 1959. Outwardly, the regime seemed to have won a runaway victory. All of its candidates, except two, were elected. Nhu had worked very hard to bring off this triumph, perhaps too hard. Anyone opposed by the Ngo Dinh clan had little chance of winning. Candidates were disqualified for the most curious legal reasons. Court action was brought against one lady because a mustache had been drawn—not by her—on one of her campaign posters! Others were not allowed to run on similarly nonsensical grounds. In some cases, their posters were ruled too large; in others, too small. No excuse was silly enough, as long as it served its purpose. The real test, of course, was whether or not the candidate was for or against Diem.

The means used to discourage opposition in the cities were fairly civilized compared to the bullying tactics employed in the outlying districts. Diem's officials in the provinces had a simple way of getting unacceptable candidates to bow out of the race. When all else failed, they were told that unless they quit they would be denounced as communists and tried before military tribunals. That was usually the end of that.

Two candidates managed to win without Nhu's endorsement. One, an independent, was judged harmless and allowed to take his seat. The other, Dr. Phan Quang Dan,

127

was not. Dr. Dan had committed two unpardonable sins. He was extremely popular with the people of Saigon, and he was critical of Diem. No other prominent figure in the country was as disliked by the Ngo Dinh family as this physician turned politician who had gone to Harvard and had an enviable reputation as a nationalist and anti-communist. It was, therefore, most galling to the regime when Dan was elected in spite of Nhu's intense efforts to prevent it. Nhu's last-ditch maneuver was to send eight thousand soldiers into Dan's district with orders to vote for the government candidate. The good doctor won handily, anyway.

Diem, however, could not allow even a single opponent to hold office, particularly one as formidable and attractive as Dr. Dan. When Dan tried to take his rightful place in the Assembly, Diem's police barred his way. Trumped-up charges were brought against him. He was accused of giving free medical treatment in order to win votes. Dan was, of course, indignant, but there was little he could do except protest. The government had its way. Dr. Dan did not get his Assembly seat. Some of his most bitter remarks afterwards were leveled at the United States for allowing Diem to get away with this and similar practices. "The only message the Americans bring," he told journalist Denis Warner, "is anti-Communism. They criticize the Communists bitterly for the very things they countenance here. . . . The sad result of this is that many South Vietnamese believe that the United States is just a bigger South Vietnam with more corruption . . . and bigger concentration camps. The Americans intervene when they want to. Why don't they intervene when moral issues are at stake? They accept military and economic responsibilities. They must also accept a moral responsibility."

Tragedy befell the courageous physician following the failure of an anti-Diem army coup in November, 1960. Dr. Dan openly admitted his complicity in the plot, even though he didn't have to. Arrest and torture followed. Two years after being jailed, Dan was finally brought to trial. Sent off to the island of Poulo Condore, the ex-French penal colony, he served about a year of the eight years of hard labor he was sentenced to by Diem's judges. He was released in 1963, along with other political prisoners, in the wake of the government's downfall.

The attempt by some army officers in November, 1960, to topple Diem came dramatically close to succeeding. After its troops seized government buildings and occupied military strongpoints, an anti-Diem junta actually held control of Saigon for twenty-four hours. But the rebels made the mistake of bargaining with Diem, instead of arresting and deposing him at once. Diem pretended to go along with the insurgents' demands. He promised faithfully that he would form a new government of "national union" that would include other parties and groups. So persuasive was Diem that his captors believed what he told them. Next morning they wished they hadn't. Soldiers loyal to the government had meanwhile arrived in the capital. They attacked the rebel positions, retook them, and the coup was over. Once again the Ngo Dinh family was saved, this time by an inept enemy.

Top American officials in Saigon had known of the rebel plan beforehand, but had said nothing to Diem about it. Obviously, this meant that they welcomed a change in the regime and had no objection to Diem's removal. Diem was incensed when he learned about this later. The American failure to inform him of the impending coup he considered an outright betrayal. After this, he became even more withdrawn and suspicious. Only brother Nhu now had his complete confidence, and would from now on grow more powerful until even Diem, it is believed, became a puppet in his hands.

The new government of John F. Kennedy took office in the United States in January, 1961. Among other critical problems left behind by the outgoing administration, it found the situation in Vietnam, which seemed to be going from bad to worse. The new President consulted many experts and asked them what should be done to win the war there. One of those he talked to was Major General Edward Lansdale, whose specialty was guerrilla warfare and insurgency. Lansdale, who had been through the fight against the communist Huks in the Philippines, believed firmly that this war could not be won merely on the military level. It was a war for the people, and only the side that had the people would come out on top.

The "great lesson" of the British experience in Malaya and of his own in the Philippines, as Lansdale was to write later, was "that there must be a heartfelt *cause* to which

129

the legitimate government is pledged, a cause which makes a stronger appeal to the people than the Communist cause. . . . When the right cause is identified and used correctly, the *anti*-Communist fight becomes a *pro*-people fight." This idea impressed the President and he tried it out on some other high officials. But Lansdale had too many opponents in the top echelons of the army and government who opposed his thesis. As a result, it was never adopted as official policy by the Kennedy regime.

For years the American ambassador in Saigon had been trying to get Diem to make long-needed reforms. But the Ngo Dinh regime took action only when it wished to, which wasn't very often. Ambassador Elbridge Durbrow, who had held the post since 1957, had tried everything he knew, from threats to promises, to budge Diem, with meager results. Besides, Diem no longer liked or trusted him. Durbrow had been one of those who had been tipped off that the army would pull a coup in 1960 and had kept quiet about it. To Diem, this was little short of treason, and Durbrow's stock, which had never been high, dropped sharply.

In March, 1961, President Kennedy appointed another ambassador to South Vietnam, thinking that perhaps a mild approach would work better than Durbrow's blunter methods. The new man in Saigon, a soft-spoken gentleman from Virginia named Frederick E. Nolting, thought he could get more out of Diem by playing his role in a low key. Nolting's diplomatic style emphasized sympathy, understanding and cooperation. He was convinced that this was the best—and only—way to deal with the proud, stubborn Diem, if one expected to achieve anything. This approach was much more to the president's liking and Mr. Nolting became a favorite at the palace.

Even brother Nhu had a kind word for him. "Mr. Nolting," he told someone privately, "is the only intelligent ambassador the Americans have sent to Vietnam." There was only one thing wrong with the ambassador's polite way of doing business with the Ngo Dinh family. It didn't work. Like Durbrow before him, Nolting accomplished little, except for more pleasant relations with the appreciative Diem. Suggestions, for the most part, were ignored, and the regime went on doing pretty much as it pleased.

The dictator of South Vietnam could not see why the

United States kept insisting that he make democratic changes. The trouble, he thought, stemmed from an American failure to understand Oriental societies, which were vastly different from those of the West. Countries like Vietnam worked best when run in the old ways. Order, virtue, and a respect for tradition—such time-honored beliefs would make his nation strong. Asians didn't need the kind of freedoms that divided people and made them weaker. Liberty was a Western disease, and Diem didn't want the Vietnamese infected by it. This was the mandarin creed, plucked out of the ancient past, and Diem, after all, was a mandarin. To him, his one-man rule was not an evil, but a necessity imposed by war and history. If he relaxed his dictatorship everything would fall apart and then there would be chaos.

The same idea was expressed in a picturesque way by Diem's sister-in-law, Madame Nhu. "If we open the window," she said, "not only sunlight but many bad things will fly in." By keeping the window shut, the Ngo Dinhs made sure that the bad things—such as democracy— would be kept out. The country would become pure and virtuous only if President Diem and his family held the power in their own hands and shared it with no one else.

Later, after he had broken with the regime, Tran Van Chuong, Madame Nhu's own father, who had been the Ambassador to the United States, would say of the ruling clan: "They are very much like medieval inquisitors who were so convinced of their own righteousness that they would burn people for their own sake, and for the sake of mankind, to save them from error and sin."

The United States was therefore fighting a lost cause when it asked Diem to act democratically, for it went against everything he believed in. Ambassador Durbrow had found that out after three fruitless years of trying. Now Nolting had the same thankless task. But the new ambassador, a sweet-tempered, reasonable man, stuck doggedly to his idea that going along with Diem would pay off in the end. The Kennedy administration finally adopted the same point of view, but not for the same reason.

What brought about its unconditional support for Diem was the situation in South Vietnam, which was moving from crisis to crisis. The war against the Viet Cong was in a bad state. As things stood now, the government's military position was slipping rapidly. The attempted coup in 1960 had shown which way the winds were blowing politically. Unless Diem was propped up at both ends, the house of Ngo Dinh and the war effort with it might go crashing down together. Something would have to be done —and soon.

President Kennedy faced several choices. One was to pull out of the country and leave it to its fate. He would not do that. Another was to arrange a "neutralist" solution, as had already been done in neighboring Laos. This would mean setting up a coalition government that included the Viet Cong. Kennedy rejected that, too. The third alternative was to support Diem—or someone else—with a program of all-out aid, and to raise the American commitment in terms of both money and personnel. After much discussion with his advisers, the President chose this latter course.

The Americans decided to stick with Diem for several reasons. In spite of his autocratic behavior, he was a man of proven courage who had become a world-wide symbol of anti-communist resistance. To replace him, they would have to find someone of equal stature, and they had no such candidate. Also, it might be dangerous and self-defeating to change regimes in midwar.

So the mandarin president stayed on and the official word went out: support Diem. But Diem himself was a little wary of his American allies by now, and with good reason. He had been given such assurances before. To show that he meant what he said, Kennedy sent Vice-President Lyndon Johnson on a goodwill trip to Saigon in the spring of 1961. Johnson told Diem that he had the full support of the United States. He also, in a speech, referred to him in glowing terms as the "Winston Churchill" of Southeast Asia.

More missions to Saigon followed that of Johnson, the most important of which was undertaken by General Maxwell Taylor, the President's personal military adviser. Out of the journey by Taylor, and the report he wrote on his findings, came a fateful decision by President Kennedy to send more American soldiers to help Diem's army fight the Viet Cong. There were about six hundred such "advisers" in the country before Kennedy's move. The President's action eventually swelled their ranks to sixteen thousand. As before, their job, as officially stated, was to train and advise, and not to fight, but that was a thin line easily crossed in the heat of battle.

Kennedy had taken the big step. He had shown the world—which included Ho Chi Minh, Mao and Khrushchev—that the United States was in Vietnam to stay. Americans began to pour into Saigon by plane and ship. Soon the capital was filled with generals, admirals and other senior officials who had been sent in as part of the crash program to win the war. The network of military and civilian agencies began to look like a monstrously large spider web that just kept spinning and adding to itself. The job of this second government in South Vietnam —for such it truly was—was to pump new life, new ideas and new effort into the floundering Diem regime and get it to work better.

Diem and Nhu were still the big bottlenecks in getting things done. The way the government was set up, nobody had the power to make decisions, neither the trivial nor the important ones, except the president. Nhu had no official position, so all policy matters—and there were many—had to be taken up directly with Diem. This inefficient, time-consuming way of running a state left the Americans limp with frustration. In addition to being turned down, as he usually was, an official calling at the palace had to sit through Diem's interminable lectures, which might be on anything from meteorology to pest extermination.

Heading the U.S. Mission in Saigon were two men, one a general, the other a civilian. General Paul D. Harkins, commander of the newly created MAC, Military Assistance Command, took care of the military end. Ambassador Nolting was in charge of civilian operations. Fortunately, both men agreed on basic strategy and liked each other, so they worked well together as a team. Like Nolting, the general took a "soft" line with Diem, which he believed to be in the best interests of his country.

As the expanded United States effort swung into high gear, it ran into an unexpected obstacle—the American newspaperman. Raised in an old tradition of freedom of the press, the journalists in Saigon reported the news as they saw it. Often this meant criticism of the regime and the way it was waging war. This incensed high Mission officials who felt that they were being stabbed in the back by the disloyal reporters. Relations between the Mission and the press grew strained and bitter. The writers resented being told that they were unpatriotic because they refused to slant the news to fit official policy needs. The Mission replied that they were already slanting the news by reporting the facts falsely.

Truth, it later developed, was on the side of the newspapermen. The Mission, in its zeal to think positively, had swallowed everything the Diem regime told it. It passed these so-called facts along to the journalists, who were expected to report them as given to their readers back home. The Mission and Diem said that the war was being won. The newsmen, however, believing only what their eyes told them, went out into the field and saw for themselves. The conclusion they drew from their observations was that if this was the way to win a war, they would hate to see one that was being lost. They also brought back with them a cynical little ditty that had been made up by American advisers working in combat areas. Sung to the tune of "Twinkle, Twinkle Little Star," it went:

> "We are winning, this we know.
> General Harkins tells us so.
> In the delta, things are rough.
> In the mountains mighty tough.
> But we're winning, this we know.
> General Harkins tells us so.
> If you doubt this is true,
> McNamara says so too."

So the feud continued. One incident in particular sheds a revealing light on the thin-skinned attitude of American officialdom toward the pesky reporters. Admiral Harry D. Felt, commander of the Pacific Fleet, was holding a news conference. One of the young newsmen present, Malcolm Browne of the Associated Press, asked the admiral a difficult question. Felt was so annoyed at Browne that instead of replying, he snapped out angrily, "Why don't you get on the team?"

If Diem was grateful for the attempts to shield him from an aroused and outraged press, he had a most peculiar way of showing it. He was certain, for instance, that the American government had something to do with the critical stories that were being written by reporters in Saigon, and that it was all part of a plot against him. Nobody could tell him that this was one of the penalties of having a free press, for he didn't believe it. In his country, the newspapers behaved themselves or they were punished. Why couldn't the United States do likewise, especially when it was in the interests of an ally during wartime? No amount of explanation could convince him that the United States government had no control over newspapers and what they printed. Diem went on believing what he wanted to.

And so it went, as the regime grew more suspicious each time its actions were challenged or questioned. Behind every criticism, it imagined a plot. It saw plotters everywhere, in the army, among the Americans, even among individuals it had once counted as close friends.

One American was suspected of being mixed up in a bizarre air attack on Diem and his family. One day, late in February, 1962, the residents of Saigon spotted two planes flying over the presidential palace. To their amazement, they saw bombs fall, followed by explosions. The pilots, out to kill Diem and Nhu, failed in their mission. The brothers were unharmed. The Nhus' Chinese governess was the only fatality. The fiery Madame Nhu was hurt when she raced to rescue her children and fell through a gaping bomb hole in the floor. By dropping most of their bombs on the wing where the Nhus lived, the fliers—both pilots in Diem's Air Force—made it quite clear who they really wanted to get. One of the planes was shot down by antiaircraft fire. But the other pilot got away, flying his damaged craft into Cambodia where he was given sanctuary.

The American accused of being involved in this strange affair was Dr. Stanley Millet, a professor who taught political science at Saigon University. Known as an open critic of the Ngo Dinhs, Millet had long been under surveillance by Nhu's secret police. The brothers, as always, looked upon any critic as a traitor and enemy. But Millet had the additional misfortune of being friendly with the father of one of the renegade pilots. Nhu was sure that he was one of the plotters in the bombing raid. Along with others who were rounded up, Millet was held by the police and questioned. Diem always believed that he was guilty, but the

135

professor, who swore his innocence, was finally released and left the country.

By 1962, Saigon was a city fully at war. The government's casualty figures kept rising. Its soldiers were dying at the rate of five hundred a month. It was losing one thousand more in wounded and captured. American helicopters flew in and out with cargoes of troops, either heading for battle or coming back. Fighters and bombers streaked through the sky day and night. The city's port was cluttered and clogged with ships bringing in goods and supplies. Its streets were filled with soldiers, more and more of them Americans.

This new breed of American fighting man—technically, an "adviser"—was getting fed up with the secrecy surrounding his role. The United States, as one of them put it, was in the war "up to our necks," so why not say so? The administration, however, for legal and diplomatic reasons, was not ready to go that far yet. Training and advising—that's all its soldiers were doing in South Vietnam. So the polite fiction persisted, though it fooled no one. It was fairly common knowledge that when Americans in the field were shot at by the Viet Cong, they shot back.

The communist guerrillas, in the meanwhile, were up to their old tricks, and some new ones. The delta land south of Saigon was their main target area in 1962. Here, among the lush rice paddies, they made their greatest gains. Fighting, raiding, murdering and politicking by night, when the government troops preferred to sleep, they moved from village to village. The peasants they won over fed them, gave them shelter, and also gave them their sons as soldiers.

The government tried to stop the red tide by building what it called "strategic hamlets." Whole communities left their old dwellings behind and moved to new fortified villages that had been erected at specially selected sites. Built by those who went to live in them, they were encircled by barbed wire, mud walls, and rows of bamboo spikes hidden in ditches and moats. The younger peasants were given arms and formed into village militia. Their job was to fight the Viet Cong when they came.

Some of the strategic hamlets did what they were supposed to do. They kept out the Viet Cong, cut off their food supply, and allowed the peasants to work in peace, with less danger of attack. But this was true only in areas where the government was still strong and could supply the hamlets with a cover of security. In territory where the government was weak, the Viet Cong made short work of the peasant defense systems. In some cases, they attacked and destroyed them by fire. In others, their agents bored from within and took them over.

The tempo of war was also accelerating in other parts of the country. A fierce struggle was being waged for the highlands of Central Vietnam. General Giap once said of this area, which is mostly mountains grown thick with jungle, "To seize and control the highlands is to solve the whole problem of South Vietnam." During 1961 and 1962, infiltrators from the north drifted into the mountain regions and stayed. There they recruited from the local tribes and began their raids on the plateaus and plains. Their aim was to set up a series of bases and then gradually absorb the whole stretch of land running from the Laotian border in the west to the sea in the east. If they succeeded, South Vietnam would be cut in half.

The Vietnamese needed all the help they could get in this critical campaign, and the Americans gave it. Their pilots flew air cover for Diem's troops. Their strategists drew up plans for winning the mountain peoples—or Montagnards—away from the Viet Cong. But halting the rebel drive was something else entirely. The enemy had made many converts among the hill folk, and as long as men and fresh supplies kept coming in from the jungle trails of Laos, they would be hard to dislodge.

For a time, the Americans made headway among the hill tribes. Camps were set up to train hillsmen to fight guerrilla fashion. The men from the hills were good fighters and gave fine accounts of themselves in combat. But the Montagnards and the Vietnamese soldiers, who came from the lowlands, were divided by a long tradition of enmity and strife.

The Montagnards were descended from the same people who had been driven into the hills more than two thousand years before by the invading Viets, and then stayed there to live. Ethnically different from the Vietnamese, they had their own languages and cultures which had hardly changed over the centuries. To the valley dwellers, who regarded them with disdain, the primitive mountaineers

137

were little more than savages. The Vietnamese, a superstitious people, had legends about evil spirits who lived in the mountains and preyed on strangers. Thus, many of Diem's soldiers did not like to fight in the hill country where there was the twin menace of the Viet Cong and the highland demons. They also found it difficult to live among the Montagnards whom they disliked and considered inferior.

The Americans could keep a lid on these hostile feelings as long as they were around to keep order. But when they weren't, there were angry squabbles that sometimes developed into real battles. What were actually small wars broke out at several camps that had been put together after months of long, hard, patient work. Then the mountain people left the camps and wandered back to their old haunts. Many such tribesmen went over to the Viet Cong, who wooed them after they broke with the government.

Above the central highlands is the northern part of South Vietnam which has some of the most difficult terrain in the world. It is, once again, an area of mountains and jungles, so treacherous in its aspects that mere human survival there would be a problem. The jungle, like a solid green wall, is virtually impenetrable, and many of its hills are steep enough to defy all but the bravest climbers. Yet here, too, there was war.

The Viet Cong had set up camps in the mountains that were hard to reach and almost impossible to attack. From these bases, they sought to penetrate the coastal areas to the east. Constant pressure was exerted on the rebels to prevent this. Government troops kept trying to get behind them and drive them down into the lowlands for a battle in the open. But the Viet Cong were too cagey to let themselves be trapped. So the war in the north went on, slowly and grimly, with the insurgents making small but steady gains, while the government fought desperately to stave them off.

Twilight had begun to settle over the regime of Ngo Dinh Diem as the year 1963 began. The president ruled in his palace like a monarch cut off from his people. Hatred of him and his family mounted until the air of Saigon seethed with it. Rumors of plots and coups swirled through the city almost daily. In these circumstances,

Diem sought only to hold on to his power. The war became secondary. Officers were promoted when they kept the casualty lists down. There was only one sure way to do that—not to fight. Not fighting became a way of life with some commanders and a way of keeping their jobs.

Diem and Nhu watched the army like a pair of hawks. In its ranks, they knew, were generals who were only waiting for an opening before they would strike. Troops known to be absolutely loyal to Diem were kept in Saigon against any such emergency. Bunkers and secret passageways were built deep in the cellars of the palace in the event a coup should come.

Inside it a mood of siege prevailed. Diem relied only on his brother now when there were major decisions to make. Nhu and his ambitious wife were at the pinnacle of power, and flaunted it openly. As the two Nhus moved into the limelight, the short, squat figure of Ngo Dinh Diem seemed to recede into the background. Crisis had brought doubt and worry to this man of once firm purpose and conviction. When he grew soft and wavered, Nhu and his acid-tongued spouse stiffened his spine. As long as they stood at the president's side, there would be no compromises. The Americans tried to separate Diem from his brother, but he would not listen. If he was destined to fall, he would fall with Nhu.

It was in the midst of this uneasy, doom-laden atmosphere that the Buddhist crisis of 1963 erupted in all its fury. A showdown between Diem and the Buddhists had been building ever since he became premier in 1954. Diem, a Catholic, naturally felt more at home with other Catholics. Many of the leading posts in the government and army were held by Catholics, who were also privileged when it came to making money out of business deals engineered by the regime.

Of the fifteen million people in South Vietnam, a little more than a million were Catholic. The rest, mainly Buddhist, resented the favoritism shown Catholics. The difference in treatment was even more blatant in the provinces where the local priests and government officials, mostly Catholics, too, were all-powerful. When strategic hamlets were built, the Catholic inhabitants were excused from working and non-Catholics were brought in to labor in their places. When new land was opened for development,

139

Catholics got the pick of the land in the safe coastal regions. The land given to Buddhists was inland, where they would have to work under the menacing shadow of the Viet Cong. Many Buddhists, seeing where the grass was greener, tried to become Catholics.

The feeling between Buddhists and Catholics had grown until, in the spring of 1963, the tense atmosphere was ripe for trouble. Early in May, in the old imperial capital of Hue, there occurred an incident that set off a national Buddhist rebellion. The issue at stake was whether or not the Buddhists would be allowed to fly their religious flags on the anniversary of the birth of Buddha 2,507 years ago. The government had banned such displays, but the Buddhists would not obey because Catholics had been allowed to fly the Vatican flag during a recent ceremony honoring Diem's brother, Archbishop Thuc.

On May 8, Buddhists staged a mass protest outside the city's radio station. Carrying flags and other religious items, they packed the narrow, alley-like streets. Ordered to disperse, they would not move. Troops under the assistant province chief, a Catholic army major, tried to scatter the crowd with tear gas and by spurting jets of water from fire hoses. But the Buddhists would not be budged. The overwrought major then made an error. He had his soldiers fire their rifles and toss grenades at the demonstrators. When the smoke cleared, nine Buddhists lay dead and many others were wounded and injured. Diem's officials later tried to blame the communists for the bloody affair. Red agitators, they said, had hurled the bombs that caused the killings. There were few, however, who believed the story.

The tragedy at Hue brought a lame promise by the government that it would start an investigation. This did not satisfy the Buddhists, who asked for an outright apology and an admission from the regime that it had been at fault. More than that, they wanted Diem to agree to certain reforms, one of which was that Buddhism be given legal status as a religion. Astonishingly, in South Vietnamese law, which was a holdover from the French period, Buddhism was described merely as an "association." Roman Catholicism, on the other hand, had official recognition as a religion.

Failure to satisfy Buddhist demands touched off a wave

140

of protests and riots. On June 1, again in Hue, during a demonstration, sixty Buddhists were badly burned by tear gas grenades—that police threw into their ranks. The single most dramatic moment of the Buddhist revolt came in Saigon on June 11. Early in the morning an old gray sedan pulled up at a street corner near the Xa Loi pagoda. Four monks got out of the car. One of them, seventy-three-year-old Thich Quang Duc, sat down on the pavement and crossed his legs. Two of the other monks raised a gasoline can and poured its contents over him. Calmly then, the old monk struck a match and was engulfed instantly in a mass of orange flames. This was the first in a series of suicides by Buddhist bonzes—or monks—that shocked the rest of the world. A famous photograph taken on the spot by reporter Malcolm Browne added to the general reaction of horror.

The United States put pressure on Diem to placate the Buddhists, but he was reluctant to do so. To give in now would be to lose face, and this the Ngo Dinh brothers would not do. Nhu and his wife were the most bitter opponents of compromise with the Buddhists. The vengeful Madame Nhu, to show her contempt, termed the fiery suicides "Buddhist barbecues," and told reporters she wished there would be more of them. Her husband said that it was all part of a plot, and that the communists were behind it. Fearing that there might indeed be communist infiltration among the Buddhists, American investigators explored the charges. No evidence turned up to support the accusation.

The crisis compelled Washington to take a firmer stand with Diem. As part of its new, tough approach, it withdrew Ambassador Nolting from his post. The new ambassador, Henry Cabot Lodge, was a former political opponent of John F. Kennedy. But the President needed someone in Saigon with iron in his back, and the veteran Lodge seemed the right man for the job.

Lodge had a long record of outstanding public service. He had been a U.S. Senator for many years, then the Ambassador to the United Nations, and most recently the Republican candidate for Vice-President in 1960. The patrician Lodge, member of a distinguished old Massachusetts family, arrived in Saigon on the evening of August 22. The American position immediately stiffened. Soon Mission officials were making joking bets with their Vietnamese friends that "our old mandarin can beat your old mandarin." The duel referred to, that between Lodge and Diem, began on a jarring note.

One day before the new ambassador flew in, brother Nhu had raided the Buddhist pagodas in Saigon. The raid was meant as a warning to Lodge that the regime would not change its Buddhist policy. It was also a direct affront to the United States and to Lodge personally. But if Nhu thought he would bully him by this action, he had picked on the wrong man.

Hundreds of Buddhist bonzes were rounded up by Nhu's night-raiding secret police. Two priests managed to vault over a pagoda wall and escape. They ran into a building that housed the U.S. Operations Mission (USOM) and asked for sanctuary. It was granted and the Buddhists stayed there for weeks as guests of the United States government. One of Ambassador Lodge's first acts after reaching Saigon was to visit the two religious refugees at the Mission, an open rebuke to Diem and Nhu. Two weeks later, three more bonzes dashed past the guards at the American embassy and requested shelter. They, too, were taken in, which led some wit to call the ambassador's residence the "Buddhist Hilton."

There was another ominous sign for the regime. The students, usually a peaceful group, also began demonstrating. University and high school students staged street marches. The government struck back by closing down the schools and arresting more than a thousand students. For days afterward, some of the saddest sights in Saigon were the bicycles piled up outside the empty schools. Nobody came to take them away and they just lay there, slowly rusting in the rain. Gradually, the youngsters were let go and returned to their anxious parents. This action was further proof, if such was needed, of the abyss that had opened up between Diem and the people.

Early in September, Madame Nhu flew off to Europe for a few weeks. Then she went to the United States for a much publicized visit. Touring the country, she made speeches, held interviews, and appeared on television. Viewers had the eerie feeling that they were looking at the Dragon Lady come to life. She was beautiful and smiling but her words, when she spoke, were caustic and sharp.

She had an unfortunate talent for saying the wrong thing at the wrong time. Instead of making friends for the hard-pressed Ngo Dinhs, as she had intended, she made more critics and enemies. From beginning to end, her American stay was an official disaster. She was still in the United States, raging against the Buddhists and "communist plots" as, back in Saigon, Diem and Nhu went through the last performance of their world-famous brother act.

Nhu, by now, was literally drunk with power. His secret police were everywhere, prying, snooping, jailing. To American officials, he confided in private that Diem was "weak" and that he, Nhu, might have to take over the government. He was also, through contacts in Hanoi, making secret peace feelers to Ho Chi Minh. Fearing that the Ngo Dinhs might be deserted by the Americans, Nhu was preparing an escape hatch.

Early in October, the United States had cut off a portion of its economic aid to South Vietnam. Some of this $12 million a month paid the salaries of Diem's soldiers and Nhu's Special Forces and secret police. Soon the squeeze would be on, for the regime could not function without these funds. President Kennedy had taken this step in a last effort to force reforms. But Diem, backed by his brother, held out stubbornly.

The Americans were aware that a plot against the brothers was about to take place. Army leaders had been in touch secretly with United States officials and told them of their plans. They had not been discouraged by the Americans, so they knew it was all right to continue. Nhu, too, suspected something. Only recently, he had summoned the country's top generals to the palace and warned them not to try a coup d'etat. Three of the men present at that session were the plot ringleaders. General Duong Van Minh —or Big Minh, as he was called—was the regime's adviser on military affairs. General Tran Van Don was the army's chief of staff, and General Le Van Kim had once commanded the National Military Academy. The generals had moved slowly and carefully as they prepared the destruction of the Ngo Dinh family. Now they were ready.

Diem and Nhu felt safe in Saigon. They had enough loyal troops on hand to fend off any coup attempt. Commanding these forces was an officer in whom they had absolute trust, General Ton That Dinh. But unknown to the brothers, Dinh had joined the plotters.

Sensing that a coup was imminent, Nhu devised a scheme to counter it. He called in Dinh and told him how his stratagem was to work. First, he was to order some of his troops out of Saigon in the pretext that they were being sent into combat. The city would thus be left virtually un-defended. Then squads of thugs, specially trained by Nhu's hirelings, would stage a fake coup. Diem and Nhu, by prearranged plan, would flee Saigon. Meanwhile, other loyal troops, as part of the ruse, would be lying in wait out-side the city. They would come storming back into Saigon, overthrow the fake coup leaders, and beg the Ngo Dinhs, for the good of the country, to take over the government again. The brothers would then return to the capital in a great show of glory and triumph, stronger and more secure than they had ever been.

Through Dinh, the real plotters got wind of this scheme. When Diem's troops moved out, as planned, the rebels struck swiftly. The first shots of the coup rang out in Sai-gon at 1:30 P.M. on Friday, November 1, in the middle of the siesta hour. The timing had been perfect, for most of the city was taking its regular midday nap. Rebel troops quickly seized vital centers—the radio station, the post of-fice, the telephone exchange, and police headquarters.

Diem and Nhu were having a leisurely lunch at the pal-ace when word reached them about the uprising. At first Nhu thought it was part of his own plan, but after he tried to reach Dinh and failed, he realized something had gone astray. This was no fake coup. When the rebels called the palace and asked Diem to surrender, he refused. Then he made his own phone call to Ambassador Lodge. What was the attitude of the United States in this situation, he wished to know? He soon found out. The ambassador, of course, knew all about the coup. Lodge told Diem that he was con-cerned about his safety and suggested that he either give up or come to the American embassy where he would be given protection. That was all. Diem knew from this conversa-tion that he could expect no further help from the Ameri-cans. The Ngo Dinhs were now on their own in a friendless world.

Diem could still have saved himself by going to the em-bassy, for the Americans had made arrangements to fly him out of the country after the coup took place. But Diem, a strange, stubborn man, did not accept Lodge's offer. His duty, he told the ambassador, was to stay at his post and try to restore order. These were the last words that passed between them. He did not call Lodge again.

The brothers made many phone calls, trying to rally support. Soldiers of the palace guard were making a brave stand against the attacking rebels, but they could not hold out much longer. Diem called his commanders; Nhu tried to reach the leaders of his own private forces. But nobody wished to join the side that had obviously lost. With each refusal, the situation became more grim. Diem still had one glimmer of hope left—Dinh. To the very end, he had believed in Dinh's loyalty. Not until late in the day, when he finally spoke to him on the phone, did he learn of Dinh's treachery. "You are finished," Dinh told him vindictively. "It is over." This was a bitter blow to Diem, who had been very fond of Dinh.

A little after dawn next morning, rebel soldiers broke into the palace. Diem and Nhu were gone. They had escaped the evening before through a tunnel in the basement and gone to the home of Ma Tuyen, a Chinese friend who lived in neighboring Cholon. All night long, Diem tried more phone calls, desperately seeking help. They were all in vain. By morning, the brothers knew that they had reached the end. After attending mass at the Catholic church next to Ma Tuyen's, Diem called rebel headquarters and surrendered.

A five-car convoy was sent to fetch the pair. When it came, Diem and Nhu were waiting on the steps of the church. Hands tied behind their backs, the prisoners were hearded into the lead vehicle of the convoy, an armored personnel carrier. Captain Nhung, an aide to General Minh, got inside the carrier with the Ngo Dinh brothers and the door closed behind them. Then the convoy drove away.

A little while later it pulled up in front of rebel headquarters. The back door of the carrier was opened. Diem and Nhu were sprawled on the floor. Both were dead. The hands of the victims were still tied behind their backs. Nhu had been stabbed several times and shot. Diem had been shot in the head.

145

Chapter 10

AN AMERICAN WAR

NGO DINH DIEM had ruled South Vietnam for almost a decade. He had been its first leader, and its life had literally begun with his rise to power. Now that his life was over, the struggling nation entered a new phase of its history. His American allies had given up reluctantly on the mandarin president. Only when they were convinced that he was leading his country to ruin and defeat did they abandon him to his enemies. But if they had hoped that the change would work a miracle in the fortunes of war and politics, they were rapidly disappointed. For what followed Diem was no great improvement, and, in many ways, even suffered by comparison with the Ngo Dinh regime. Instead of the longed-for stability, there was continuing chaos and unrest. Instead of unity, there was division and rivalry. Instead of victory, there was more defeat.

Slowly, the realization sank in that the Vietnam war was in danger of turning into an American war. Without the Americans, South Vietnam would have crumbled long ago. Only American money, American arms, and American power were keeping the stricken land on its feet. This was a situation the United States had tried to avoid. It was *their* war, President Kennedy had said, meaning the South Vietnamese, and *they* would have to win it. All the Americans could do was help. But what if the South Vietnamese could not win it by themselves? What would happen then? Would the United States accept the verdict of history, bow out of the picture and depart? Or would it make another decision —to stand and fight, no matter what?

One man would be making that choice, if and when it came to that, and he sat in the White House in Washington, thousands of miles away from the fighting and dying —the President of the United States. John F. Kennedy had been shaken by Diem's brutal death, which he deplored and regretted. Yet only three weeks later, he, too, would be lying dead in Dallas, Texas, the victim of an assassin's bullet. Lyndon Johnson became the new President. All the burdens and problems of this great office were now his to carry and to ponder and to solve if he could. Of them all, Vietnam—the little war that had grown—would become his biggest headache.

In South Vietnam, the people were still in shock from the suddenness and the savagery of the early November events. The power of the Ngo Dinhs was no more. After so long, it was hard to believe. Vengeance was still being taken against members of the family, when they could be found. Ngo Dinh Can, the hated ruler of Central Vietnam, was seized, tried, and later executed. Others in the clan escaped simply because they were not in the country. Madame Nhu, safe in the United States, cursed the fates that had made her a widow and brought down her brother-in-law. Also out of reach were Archbishop Thuc and Ngo Dinh Luyen, who were in Europe.

Saigon, after Diem's downfall, had celebrated. Mobs ran through the streets tearing down pictures of the late president. A giant statue erected by Madame Nhu was toppled and smashed. Newspapers that had followed the government line were raided and burned. Members of Nhu's secret police fled their homes to avoid the wrath of those they had wronged. The prisons were opened and men came out to tell grisly stories of death and torture. Night clubs, closed down by order of Madame Nhu, opened their doors for business. Once again msuic blared and dancers danced, far into the morning hours.

The city's festive air, however, told only part of the story. There was still a war going on, and it was the Viet Cong, as usual, which did most of the fighting and winning.

After the coup, the communists started a new drive in the deltas south of Saigon. Like Diem before them, General Minh and his military junta were powerless to stop the guerrillas. More territory fell into enemy hands, and the government was left with little else but the big towns and the highways.

The victorious generals ruled through a twelve-man Military Revolutionary Council. The new premier—the office of president had been abolished—was Nguyen Ngoc Tho, who had been vice-president under Diem. It was General Minh, however, and the other officers on the Council who wielded the real power. The Americans hoped that Minh would become the leader of the group, someone the people would rally around and follow. But the burly general held back from taking over. He had a great fear of being called a dictator. South Vietnam had just rid itself of one tyrant. Minh didn't want to become a new one.

While he hesitated, the country drifted. Minh was a good general but a poor politician. Neither he nor his associates knew how to run a government. Under their haphazard reign, the country floundered. The religious question had stirred again. This time it was the Catholics who complained that they were being persecuted. The economy was in a mess. Prices kept going up, that of rice especially. There were strikes and student demonstrations. The war effort, too, was stalled at dead center as the generals failed to move vigorously even in this area.

The new junta lasted a little less than three months. On January 30, 1964, it was overthrown by another band of military plotters led by General Nguyen Khanh. A flamboyant character, Khanh wore a beret, sported a goatee beard, and fancied himself a man of destiny. But he, too, encountered difficulties.

Khanh had himself declared premier and tried to run both the government and the army. In the jungle of Saigon politics, this was a hopeless assignment. Constantly beset by crisis, Khanh had a hard time just keeping his job. The year during which he held power was one of the most hectic in South Vietnam's history. Several times, he resigned or was forced out of office, only to return almost at once. The shuffling around of officials, with each change of government, was enough to make an onlooker's head buzz. During this period, Khanh's official titles included those of

Premier, Commander of the Armed Forces Council, and, briefly, President, when he tried to become a dictator and failed. In between Khanh's stewardship, several civilians had brief flings at the premiership: Dr. Nguyen Xuan Oanh and Tran Van Huong.

When Khanh first took over, the Americans had high hopes for him. Everyone breathed optimism, from the highest official to the lowest. This young, energetic general was just the strong man the country lacked and needed. Secretary of Defense Robert S. McNamara, after one of his quick visits, acclaimed him as the leader who would set things right. Khanh tried to live up to his reputation. He made a great show of dash and bustle as he sped around the country by plane. He went out and met the people, argued with politicians and students, conferred with experts, and, behind the scenes, intrigued endlessly to thwart his enemies and stay in power.

And what of the war? That was still being fought in the same old places, in the same old ways, with the same old results; the Viet Cong was winning and the government was losing, though to hear some Americans talk one would have thought it was the other way around. Growing in strength and audacity, the enemy kept inflicting severe losses on the South Vietnamese army, whose morale sank lower and lower.

There were reports, however, that the communists were having their own troubles. They had suffered high casualties, too, and their rest camps in Cambodia and Laos were said to be crowded with wounded. The war, like any other war, ate up men on both sides, and they had to be replaced.

Troops from the north continued to filter in by way of the Ho Chi Minh Trail. By now, however—in mid-1964—Ho had just about run out of retrained southerners to send back to their old home bases. The new contingents of troops that arrived were almost all native North Vietnamese. Locally, though, the Viet Cong was having a hard time recruiting. In some places the pickings were so lean that they had to take boys of fourteen.

The monsoon rains come during the summer in Asia. The modern, mechanized army falters and bogs down in this period of daily, drenching storm. But guerrillas don't need wheels. They travel on foot. The Viet Cong liked to fight in monsoon weather; the government troops didn't.

149

Late in June, as the rains fell heavily, the guerrilla armies began strong offensives in every major sector of operations, in the southern deltas, the central highlands, and in the mountainous north. Hit hard, government troops at first stood fast, even winning a few notable victories in the early battles. Then, as the enemy continued to press, the South Vietnamese fell back into their old style of retreat and defeat. July was a month of bitter setbacks in which the military picture darkened even more.

July was also a month of reverses for Premier Khanh who tried to recoup his losses, both political and military, by calling for an attack on North Vietnam. In this way he sought to get the people behind him and to confuse his enemies who were gathering around for the kill. The new American ambassador, General Maxwell Taylor, did not take kindly to Khanh's belligerent pronouncements. Taylor had assumed the post only a month before, after Henry Cabot Lodge had resigned and returned to the United States. A new presidential campaign was in the offing, and Lodge had returned to the political wars on the outside chance that he might get the Republican nomination. Now Taylor, a plain-speaking, tough-minded man, had come to fill the gap, bringing with him U. Alexis Johnson, a top-notch foreign service officer as his deputy ambassador, and General William C. Westmoreland as a replacement for General Paul Harkins.

Taylor told Khanh to tone down his fighting words, and he did somewhat, though he obviously resented what he considered outside interference. Then came a series of occurrences, so remarkable in their timing that many said jokingly that Khanh must have arranged them personally. On August 2, on the heels of the Khanh-Taylor clash, an American destroyer, the *Maddox* was set upon by several North Vietnamese "PT" boats. The onslaught, which was repelled, took place in the Gulf of Tonkin, thirty miles off the coast of North Vietnam. Two days later, the *Maddox* and another destroyer were once more fired on by Ho's "mosquito fleet." This time the American warships, assisted by naval aircraft, sent two of the attackers to the bottom.

The sea assaults, seemingly out of the blue, were probably in reprisal for raids against North Vietnamese coastal radar installations on July 30, three days before the first Gulf of Tonkin incident. North Vietnam said that American warships had ventured inside the legal twelve-mile limit and raked its shores with gunfire. The United States denied the charge, though it later came out that such shellings had taken place and that the real raiders were South Vietnamese patrol boats manned by American-trained crews. United States warships had been present but they had merely stood by without firing a shot. It was never clearly explained why the American vessels were there in the first place and why, in some instances, they were only six miles from land.

If Ho, by ordering his "navy" to strike back, meant to find out what the American response would be, he soon received an answer. For two straight days, on August 4 and 5, American planes, launched from carriers, bombed and strafed four of his torpedo boat bases, causing heavy damage. Twenty-five vessels were sunk, port facilities were destroyed, and a big oil depot went up in smoke. On August 7, both houses of Congress passed a resolution authorizing the President to take "all necessary measures to repel or prevent aggression in Southeast Asia." These broad powers were virtually a blank check for Lyndon Johnson to fill in whenever he thought the situation demanded it. In effect, it gave him permission to go to war without asking Congress, even though, under the Constitution, it was the Congress and not the President that had the war-making power.

Six months later, the President showed that he fully understood the powers he had been given and that he knew how to use them. In a sneak night attack, on February 7, the Viet Cong hit the airbase at Pleiku in the central highlands. Airplanes and helicopters were blasted and ripped by mortar fire. The American barracks, another target, was also rocked by an explosive barrage. After the guerrillas fled, the Americans counted their losses. Eight soldiers were dead, 125 more wounded. The smoldering remains of aircraft lay in twisted, misshapen piles in the hangars and on the runways.

In Washington, when he heard the news, Lyndon Johnson was grim. The raid, he knew, had been the work of the local Viet Cong; but the orders for it had most certainly come from the north. Now Johnson gave his own orders: bomb the north. The green light was flashed to his commanders in Vietnam. Only hours after the attack on Pleiku, forty-nine navy planes roared toward the North Vietnamese military base at Dong Hoi, dropped their bombs, shot up the long, gleaming rows of barracks, and sped back to their waiting carriers. Just the other side of the 17th parallel, Dong Hoi was a major staging area for troops which were being sent south for duty with the Viet Cong.

Johnson's action was a warning. Each time an American installation was assaulted, the bombers would fly north. The Viet Cong—and their northern allies—took up the challenge. Three days later they struck at the coastal base of Quinhon in Central Vietnam. Twenty-one officers and men were killed. Again the bombers took off—160 of them this time—and dropped their lethal cargoes on selected targets. Then came another unexpected American move. On February 18, for the first time, United States bombers and fighters flew combat sorties against the Viet Cong on South Vietnamese territory. From all this, observers sensed that the war was entering a different phase, as indeed it was.

It was still largely a South Vietnamese affair, although that would soon be changed. Since the middle of 1964, when the first North Vietnamese started coming in, the government's fortunes had slipped until they were now at their lowest ebb. Cocky, confident, and still growing, the Viet Cong readied themselves for the final stages of conflict. It was doubtful if the army of South Vietnam, tired and dispirited as it was, could stand up by itself much longer.

There was a sense of urgency in Washington as the President and his advisers discussed the gloomy prospects. Everything the Americans had tried so far, from Eisenhower to Kennedy to Johnson, hadn't worked. The costs of war and economic aid had grown to a staggering two million dollars a day. There were thirty thousand military advisers in the country, from a previous low of six hundred. None of the pet schemes of the Pentagon planners had yielded the miracles expected of them. Counter-insurgency had failed; pacification programs had brought few lasting results. The Americans had even, for years, been parachuting South Vietnamese terror squads into North Vietnam, but that was supposed to be a secret. All that these efforts had accomplished to date was to slow down the rate at which South Vietnam was losing the war.

As for the enemy, they were growing even more powerful and dangerous. The number of regular army North

Vietnamese soldiers infiltrating the south had reached alarming proportions, and more were streaming in. It was clear from this that Ho and his comrades were now ready to play a more active role in the southern insurgency. To revolutionary war experts, there were other signs, too, that the communists were getting ready to change over to mobile warfare, as called for by the Maoist timetable for victory. The ultimate danger point had now been reached. The war, as currently fought, was being lost. If nothing was done to turn the tide the other way, South Vietnam would soon be beyond rescue.

So a decision was made—officially called "escalation"—to raise the war to a higher, hotter level. The bombers that had flown north only in retaliation would now be turned loose on a regular basis. United States combat troops would also be sent into South Vietnam to guard American bases and to engage the Viet Cong on the ground. Step by step, through the years, the United States had moved closer to the edge of conflict. Now the armed struggle in Vietnam was about to become what many had hoped it would never be—an American war.

By bombing the north, the Pentagon planners expected to maul it so badly that Ho would be forced to call off the war and negotiate. On February 28, the bombers began their daily runs northward. The targets were restricted to military objectives and to the roads, bridges and railroads that were used to transport men and supplies heading south.

The first American combat units, 3,500 Marines, came ashore at Danang on March 8. Their job was to guard the giant airbase there and to hunt down the Viet Cong in the surrounding areas. These search-and-destroy missions, minor actions at first, were officially described as "offensive patrolling for defensive purposes." Later, they would grow more ambitious, and sweeping operations would be launched in territory long written off as communist strongholds.

What did the South Vietnamese think about these new developments? The government, the army, and loyal elements of the population were very much in favor of the air attacks, which struck back at the hated, hidden foe in the north. For the first time in years, the talk in Saigon became filled with hope. The aggressive display by the United

153

States was like tonic to a people who had been given little to cheer about before the bombings of the north began.

But the attitude of the Vietnamese switched sharply with the arrival of more American soldiers. The United States had not informed its ally, officially, that it was sending in combat forces. The maneuver was carried out, so to speak, behind the government's back. Knowing that the Vietnamese, a proud people, might object to this kind of intervention, the Americans had kept quiet about their plans. The premier of South Vietnam had learned about the troop landings at Danang in the same way that less exalted citizens did, through press announcements.

Not unexpectedly, there were immediate outcries and protests. Even though he was there to help, the American, like any other foreigner, was viewed with suspicion. This distrust of the outsider, it must be remembered, was nothing new, having once been the state policy of the old emperors. Memories of French colonialism were still fresh in the minds of the people, and they were wary of falling under the domination of a new master. Injured pride also played its part, for the coming of the Americans told them plainly that they had failed and had to be saved by others. The common complaint, as voiced by army officers, university students and intellectuals was, "the Americans are running the whole show."

In the United States, too, there were loud objections, but of another kind. Ever since 1961, when President Kennedy had nailed down the American commitment in Vietnam, worried voices had been raised about the United States role there. Now, after Johnson's bold move, the anti-war sentiment took hold and swept across the country. The antagonists to the President's policy were split up into various groups. Some were pacifists who were opposed to fighting in any war. A few—mostly far leftists—were frankly in favor of a triumph by the Viet Cong. The majority of the critics, though, were simply against American involvement in what they said was a civil war between Vietnamese. Moreover, they called both warring camps undemocratic and said that the United States was wrong in backing one side against the other. Their greatest fear was that as the war grew, Russia and China would intervene, too. This would lead to something no American strategists wanted

—a major land war in Asia that might explode into nuclear conflict.

Those who supported the government's stand thought that the communists had to be stopped in Asia and that Vietnam was the right battleground for it. Among themselves, however, they held differing views about how this was to be done. Some said that Johnson's course, a show of limited force, was the only way to halt communist aggression and still keep Russia and China out of the fight. But this position did not satisfy a more militant minority who would not accept anything less than total victory. Its adherents were ready to supply as many ground troops as were needed, to bomb the cities and industrial centers of North Vietnam, and even to use nuclear weapons, if necessary.

A bitter quarrel broke out between the "doves" and the "hawks," as the anti- and pro-war factions were popularly known. Meetings were held in universities throughout the United States—the so-called "teach-ins"—at which opponents debated each other in marathon sessions that sometimes lasted for days. Eminent people spoke for both viewpoints—writers, professors and political experts of great reputation. Dealing with the same sets of facts, they arrived at opposite conclusions, sharply and often angrily. There were also demonstrations and marches against the war in some of the larger cities. Not since the fevered days preceding World War II, when the "isolationists" and their foes hammered at each other, had a question so divided the country. Then, the issue—whether or not to get mixed up in Europe's affairs—had also been one of war or peace.

Lyndon Joynson had been just a young congressman then, learning the political ropes under President Franklin D. Roosevelt. He had been a good pupil and had come far. As an astute politician, Johnson always kept a sharp ear tuned to public opinion. Now, by raising the stakes in Vietnam, he had stirred up a storm of controversy. The war cries of the hawks and the horror of the doves were signs to him that a middle ground had to be found upon which the whole country could stand. Johnson had rattled the sword in February and March. On April 7, in a memorable address at Johns Hopkins University in Baltimore, he changed his tone and spoke in softer accents of reason and statesmanship.

155

First, he restated the American intent to safeguard the freedom of South Vietnam and to repel the communist grand design of conquest and subversion in Asia. Then he held out the olive branch of peace to his enemies. ". . . The only path for reasonable men," he said, "is the path of peaceful settlement," and called, dramatically, for "unconditional discussions" to end the war. More than that, he offered one billion dollars of American money to finance an economic development program in Southeast Asia that would help all countries in that region, including North Vietnam. He also promised American "farm surpluses to assist in feeding and clothing the needy in Asia."

Reactions to the Johnson speech varied. The response in the United States, and the West, generally, was favorable. Hanoi and Peking, the two communist capitals of Asia, termed it insincere and dishonest. They also dismissed Johnson's billion-dollar aid scheme as a flagrant attempt to "bribe" them. In South Vietnam, the speech had a mixed reception. Between words of praise by the premier and other high government officials, there had been a note of worry about Johnson's use of the phrase "unconditional discussions," which they felt had opened the door to negotiations.

That was the last thing the South Vietnamese leaders wanted. They had no doubt that North Vietnam's ultimate goal was to swallow up the south, and they feared that negotiations now would be the first step leading in that direction. They wanted no deals with the communists until the military balance had shifted in their favor and the beaten Ho would have to call it quits in South Vietnam. And from the way things were going now, that was still a long way in the future.

Politically, the country was still in a snarl, but at least the chaotic rule of General Khanh was over. That unpredictable officer had been ousted for good by a coup on February 20 and sent into exile abroad. The new junta of generals put in a civilian as premier, the well-known Dr. Phan Huy Quat. This was, incidentally, the ninth regime since the death of Diem, only fourteen months before. Quat, like the others, was given little chance of success. The quicksand quality of political life in South Vietnam would suck him under just as it had his predecessors. What hope could there be for stable government in this brawling arena where premiers came and went like figures spun through a revolving door? There were too many contenders for power, who never seemed able to get together —Catholics against Buddhists, civilian politicians against the military, young generals against old generals, mountain people against lowland dwellers, the city against the countryside, region against region. . . . Nobody seemed able to find the key to this vexing dilemma, and governments fell as fast as they were formed.

Quat's tenure, predictably short, lasted a little over three months. He was overturned, finally, after a bitter row with the Catholics who accused him of wanting a negotiated peace, something they opposed violently. Quat tried to iron out the dispute but failed. As a last resort, he asked the country's military leaders to act as go-betweens and try to work out a settlement. The same generals who had made him premier in February now decided that the weary Dr. Quat had outlived his usefulness. On June 12, under pressure, he resigned. Seven days later, the military junta announced the name of the new premier they had selected. He was Marshal Nguyen Cao Ky, thirty-four-year-old commander of South Vietnam's air force.

To help Ky rule was a committee of generals known simply as the Directory. Most of its ten members, like the premier, were young men. The older generals had been shunted off to the sidelines and were no longer running things. Ky, a dashing, handsome officer, had absolutely no political experience. Before taking office, he had been his country's number one flyer and something of a playboy. Now he had to settle down and try to learn the fine points of government and statecraft. American officials crossed their fingers and hoped that he would have better luck than all the other post-Diem premiers. It was a lot to ask for.

Ky took office under trying conditions. The war had reached a new low and the gloom in Saigon was thicker than fog. The communists, as feared, had shifted to tactics of mobile warfare, which were paying off handsomely already. Following the Maoist rulebook to the letter, they lashed out in strength all along the line. Now, in a series of probing thrusts, they were throwing whole battalions and regiments at the reeling South Vietnamese. As the summer rainy season approached, strategists watched these

157

Viet Cong tuneups with mounting concern. Soon, they knew, when the rains came, the big monsoon offensives would begin.

Even in these preliminaries, the guerrillas had scored impressive triumphs, topped by a stunning win at Dong Xoai, which lay fifty-five miles to the north of Saigon. There, a Special Forces fort manned by South Vietnamese had been blitzed and overrun by two Viet Cong regiments. The defenders, three battalions strong, had been wiped out almost to a man. It was the war's fiercest battle so far and the south's biggest defeat.

The Americans, too, felt the fury of the communist charge. At Duc Co and Bu Dop, near the Cambodian border, U.S. Special Forces (the famous Green Berets) were slashed and roughed up by regiment-sized assaults. The immediate outlook became so bleak that General Westmoreland, commanding officer of the slowly expanding American force, put in a hurry-up call to Washington for help. The President went into an eight-day huddle with his staff and, in July, came out of it with a beefed-up version of his original plan that sent planes and soldiers into Vietnam at a sharply accelerated rate. The quota of troops was raised from 75,000 to 125,000; monthly draft calls were more than doubled from 17,000 to 35,000.

Almost at once, the American war machine raced into high gear. As troops and material poured in, new installations mushroomed into existence almost overnight. Camps and towns were gouged out of the jungles. Giant airbases with two-mile runways joined others already built. These mammoth enclaves, strung out from north to south along the curving coastline, were more than just airfields. Equipped to handle incoming ships and their cargoes, each was also a fortress, so strongly protected by land, sea and air defenses that no enemy attack could seriously breach them. They had an offensive function, too, as jumping-off points for combat teams of men and helicopters that would go scouting inland for the slippery Viet Cong guerrillas.

American strength was concentrated where it would do the most good. The marines—45,000 of them—held down the northern sector around Hue, Danang and Chu Lai. The 1st Cavalry, a newly formed outfit, took up positions at An Khe, astride the road controlling passage to the pivotal central highlands. Guarding the eastern end of the same highway, at Quinhon on the coast, were fifteen thousand men of the Capital Division, South Korea's contribution to the Vietnam war.

Further down the coast was Cam Ranh Bay, where nature itself had carved out a superb harbor. During the Russo-Japanese War of 1904-5, a huge Russian fleet had paused there briefly before it was routed in a famous sea battle off the Japanese-owned island of Tsushima. Now United States engineers had turned it into a bustling port whose sprawling facilities, still growing, required the services of 12,600 men. Its importance to the war can be measured by the following simple statistic. From this vital supply artery comes all the material used by half the American troops and many of South Vietnam's as well.

Moving south from Cam Ranh Bay, all the way down into the jungles around Saigon, the reinforcements Westmoreland had asked for were already in action. The 101st Airborne Brigade, a strike force operating from its coastal base, kept a sharp, prowling lookout for guerrillas. On jungle duty, up to the same business, were the 1st Infantry Division, the 173rd Airborne, and some token forces sent by Australia and New Zealand.

Major battles flared as the Americans sought out the enemy. Below Chu Lai, five thousand marines, in a campaign tagged "Operation Starlight," accounted for seven hundred communist dead. In mid-October, at Plei Me in the central highlands, a Special Forces camp of four hundred mountain men and twelve Americans was charged by six thousand Viet Cong. Nine days later, the attackers broke off their siege and fled. American planes, flying some six hundred separate strikes, had saved the day and killed 850 guerrillas. But for them, the defenders at Plei Me would have been annihilated.

In hot pursuit of the retreating Viet Cong went members of the 1st Cavalry Brigade. They were almost in Cambodia, in the lower hills of the rugged Chu Pong mountain mass, when they were ambushed. The trapped and badly outnumbered Americans were bailed out by the artillery men and the Air Force, but not before they had been ripped and shredded in a series of bloody skirmishes. Straggling out of the mountains afterward, they forded the Ia Drang River and ran into another ambush. A bitter battle in the tall elephant grass ended only after the guerrillas had been raked into retreat by strafing jets and flaming napalm bombs. The two engagements had taken a heavy toll on both sides: 1,200 communists were slain; 240 Americans were killed, and an additional 470 were wounded, by far the highest United States losses of the war.

In less than two months, Westmoreland had blunted the Viet Cong drive and put them on the defensive. American ground and air action inside South Vietnam had cost the enemy a total of seven thousand men. Also, the danger-filled monsoon season had come and gone, without even one victory being recorded by the communists. The jubilant commanding general could rightly call it, as he did, "an unprecedented victory."

And yet—the underlying problems remained. It was not enough to kill guerrillas and defeat them in isolated encounters. The areas fought in had to be held afterwards and ruled, and this the government was usually unable to do. So after the Americans left, as one officer put it, the communists "seeped back in like water through a wet rag." The bombings on southern soil had also left many villagers angry and resentful, for they were often the pitiful, though unintended, victims of such air attacks.

Other bitter facts also had to be faced. Despite their high casualties, the Viet Cong had more than doubled their forces from 103,000 at the beginning of 1965 to 230,000 at its end. They had done this even though they had lost an estimated 34,000 dead and 11,000 captured in the same period. As the Americans had escalated and grown in strength, the communists had kept pace by adding to their ranks. The number of infiltrators coming in each month was now 2,500, twice what it had been previously. The flow had been speeded up by three more trails hewn out of the Laotian wilderness. Stationed as guards along these routes were ten thousand men. Screened off from aerial view by trees that towered 150 feet high, they enabled caravans of soldiers, porters, trucks and elephants to move in relative safety toward the different crossing points into the South.

The bombings of North Vietnam had not brought Ho to his knees, as it had been predicted they would. Nor had they forced him to negotiate. If anything, they seemed to have stiffened the north's will to resist. When the bombings first started in February, American officials in Saigon had forecast that peace talks would be under way by September. It had not worked out that way. In July, a defiant Ho had stated, "We are determined to fight on till final victory even if we have to go on fighting for another five years, ten years, twenty years or even longer."

As the year drew to a close, the United States unleashed a new offensive—this time for peace. At Christmas, a time of traditional truce, both sides stopped fighting. The Americans, too, kept their bombers grounded during the lull. When hostilities began again, the bombers did not take to the air. As the days passed and they remained grounded, it became clear that Lyndon Johnson was up to something new and dramatically different. His critics had long been after him to halt the raids on the north. They argued that bombs had not brought Ho to the conference table, but perhaps a cessation of bombing would. It would also be a signal to the north that the United States really wanted peace and was acting in good faith. Even if it didn't work, they said, it was worth the try.

For thirty-seven days, the bombers stayed in their hangars. During that time, United States diplomats and emissaries, on whirlwind tours of the world's capitals, sought vainly to set the wheels of negotiation in motion. But the only response that came from Hanoi was one of insult and disbelief. "U.S. leaders want war and not peace," Ho Chi Minh had said at the beginning of Johnson's peace drive. Later, Ho called the American move an "impudent threat" and said that peace would come only when the Viet Cong and its National Liberation Front were accepted "as the sole genuine representative of the people of South Vietnam."

By the end of January, the President had had enough. Calling his congressional leaders into conference at the White House, he explained that the bid for peace had failed, even though he had attempted "everything humanly possible" to get Hanoi to negotiate. To emphasize the point, Secretary of State Dean Rusk, sitting at the President's side, said that thirty-eight separate efforts had been made to contact Hanoi but all had failed. When the Russians had tried to cooperate in some of these ventures, they, too, had been rebuffed.

Meanwhile, the north had used the pause to its own

good advantage. Reconnaissance photos showed huge labor armies hard at work repairing the damage that had been wrought by the year-long bombings. Railroads, bridges and highways that had been torn up or destroyed were back in working order. Bristling new antiaircraft defenses installed in vital target zones would now make it harder and more dangerous for pilots to accomplish their missions. The infiltration rate had gone up in the interim, some estimates running as high as six thousand for the preceding month. The North Vietnamese were also bringing in weapons with higher firepower, particularly mortars, that were even deadlier than those possessed by the Americans. The most shocking announcement of all came from Vice Admiral William Raborn, head of the CIA, who warned that the communists were now in the planning stage of a massive spring offensive in which Korea-style "human wave" tactics would be used. In short, while the United States had been pursuing peace, Ho and the Viet Cong had been busy preparing for a long war.

Most of the important members of Congress present, with a few exceptions, rose to assure the President that he had their full support if he decided to go back to the bombings. He, in his turn, before closing the meeting, read to them a passage from a book he had brought with him, the final volume of Bruce Catton's Civil War history, *Never Call Retreat,* which told how another President had faced up to his agonizing duties more than a century ago.

Peering down through his spectacles, Lyndon Johnson intoned it slowly and solemnly: "He had told a friend that all of the responsibilities of the Administration 'belong to that unhappy wretch called Abraham Lincoln' and as he tried to meet those responsibilities the last thing he needed or wanted was a contrived or enforced harmony. Precisely because he was leading a divided country he needed diverse counsels. He had his own grave doubts about the era that lay ahead, and so did most of his fellow citizens, and the true strength of his leadership had to arise from his ability to work out his doubts as he went along. Only so could he hope to carry all factions with him."

Later that weekend, as he gave the word for the bombers to fly north again, the President knew that his action would let loose a new wave of dissent throughout the country. The anti-war sentiment had been gaining, rather

162

than losing, ground and had even reached into the chambers of the House of Representatives and the Senate. Most outspoken in their opposition were two senators from the President's own party: the grave, courtly, scholarly J. William Fulbright of Arkansas and the fiercely independent Wayne Morse of Oregon. Both were influential members of the Senate Foreign Relations Committee, which had recently opened a series of sensational hearings on Vietnam. The testimony before the Committee made headlines for weeks and gave the whole country an opportunity to study the differences in views and opinions between those who upheld the government's position and those who opposed it. Testifying for the government were two of its stalwarts, Secretary Rusk and General Maxwell Taylor. Critical of the official policy, though in different ways, were former Ambassador George F. Kennan, and General James M. Gavin.

Both of these critics were men of great reputation and achievement who had served their country with distinction before returning to private life. Kennan, a foreign policy expert and Pulitzer Prize-winning historian, was known for his brilliance and forceful opinions. And in General Gavin, an officer risen from the ranks, the army had produced a top military planner with a first-rate mind to match. These credentials gave added weight to the points of view expressed by the diplomat and the general at the hearings.

The main thrust of their criticism was that the Administration's Vietnam policy was endangering the national interest and not serving it. Ambassador Kennan called for a scaling down of existing military and political programs to meet the realistic needs of the situation. The goal of such a modified policy, he believed, should be to create the basis for a negotiated settlement. General Gavin's much talked about "enclave" theory stated this position primarily in military terms—to withdraw from territories where the Viet Cong were too strong and hold on to politically reliable areas that could be maintained and defended with fewer soldiers and supplies, and at far less cost. These sanctuaries—or enclaves—would be set up mainly in and around the cities, but also at key military installations and loyal rural communities.

The shared view of both Kennan and Gavin was that it

would be self-defeating and increasingly dangerous if the United States continued on its present course and tried to resolve the Vietnam dilemma by military means alone. The pure application of force in slowly growing doses could only lead to runaway escalation and all the larger risks that such a strategy entailed.

The echoes of the debate did not stop at the doors of the Senate chambers. Inside the government, too, there were said to be divisions, some taking a hawkish stand, others inclining to be more dovelike. The hawks favored greater bombings, a Korea-style buildup of combat troops, and urged the reserves be called up. These measures would show the communists that the Americans meant business and were in the fight to stay. Reputed to be in their ranks were the Joint Chiefs of Staff, Dean Rusk and Henry Cabot Lodge, who was back in Saigon again as Ambassador.

The doves had not wanted the bombings to start up again. They were also for cutting down the fighting on the ground so that there would be less danger of a clash with Red China. In their judgment, this was the best way to bring about negotiations and end the war. McGeorge Bundy, adviser to the President, and Under Secretary of State George W. Ball were supposed to be members of this group.

Lyndon Johnson had lent an ear to the counsel of both wings and then had gone his own way, trodding the middle path, as usual. Now he had another problem to deal with—the shaky Ky regime in Saigon. How could the South Vietnamese fight and win a war if the political ground kept shifting under them all the time? One of these days, the governmental underpinnings would collapse altogether, and along that road lay disaster.

There had to be a way to put Ky and the war effort on a more solid footing. Johnson thought he knew how. Barely a week after he had ordered the resumption of bombing, he hastily summoned a conference between himself and Premier Ky at Honolulu in Hawaii. It was a full-dress affair, replete with all the trimmings of pomp and ceremony. The President brought along almost his whole Cabinet and scores of other assistants, generals and experts. Ky arrived with General Nguyen Van Thieu, the chief of state, and a similar, though not as splendid, retinue. For three days, beginning on February 5, Johnson and the premier of South Vietnam held talks.

The President had two basic aims at this surprise government-to-government get-together. One was to bolster Ky personally, and to shore him up politically, by backing him with the full prestige of the American Presidency. This, he hoped, would help South Vietnam attain a stable political order. His other objective was to review the military picture, come to some agreements about it, and also to work out improved social and economic programs that would "win the people" over for Ky and his junta of generals.

To Johnson, this was the heart of the matter and the most important part of the conference. His advisers had told him that there were two ways to win the war against the Viet Cong. One was to use unlimited force. That was the quick, military way. The other was a "rural pacification" plan that would cost much more money and take five years or more to accomplish. The President had no hesitation in making up his mind. He had chosen the second course because it offered the more permanent and humane solution. All that remained was to put the plan into practice. But that—if the past was any measuring rod—would take a lot of doing.

The aftermath of Honolulu was not what Lyndon Johnson had hoped for. In the United States, when a politician wants to win votes, he asks the President to appear on the same platform with him. It works, too. At Honolulu, Johnson had tried the same trick with Premier Ky. There was only one flaw in his scheme. The Vietnamese people, who have become increasingly anti-American, don't like to see their leaders identified too openly with the foreigners. It makes them suspicious and leads to the belief that they are really puppets.

Johnson's public hug and endorsement was something that Ky found hard to live down when he got back to Saigon. It had also given him some big ideas about himself. Now that he had the President's blessing, Ky thought he could move safely against his other rivals for power. First and foremost on the list was General Nguyen Chan Thi, his archfoe inside the ten-man ruling Directory. General

165

Thi, commander of the army's First Corps, controlled five provinces in the north, which he dominated in the manner of an old-time warlord.

Before dismissing Thi, the premier had cleared the action with Ambassador Lodge, who told him to go ahead. Then, on March 10, Ky pushed a vote through the Directory that fired Thi. Two days later, there were anti-Ky demonstrations in Danang, Thi's headquarters, where he was very popular. The Buddhists, also friendly to Thi, began to raise their heads. As the unrest blazed up, riots, marches and strikes took place. Thich Tri Quang, leader of the more militant Buddhists, quickly stepped to the center of events.

This clever, slippery monk had been a shadowy but forceful figure in Saigon politics for years. His object, most observers agreed, was to make himself the power broker in South Vietnam's troubled political world, the man, in short, who could make or break governments. Already he had helped topple six regimes, including that of Ngo Dinh Diem. Now he was at it again, whipping up his followers, and demanding the end of military rule. In an interview with a *New York Times* correspondent, Tri Quang said the Ky administration was "rotten" and that Ky himself was "more hated" than ever since President Johnson had given him his official blessing at Honolulu.

As the crisis deepened, the government lost control of the northern provinces where the deposed General Thi was still strong. Army units, loyal to Thi, were in command at the cities of Danang and Hue, and stood ready to fight if challenged. A new civil war seemed about to erupt, which would present the incredible spectacle of two such conflicts going on in the same country at the same time—one in the cities and the other in the countryside.

The tension was eased when Ky appeared to bow to the Buddhist demands that free elections be held in the near future. Tri Quang called off his protests and demonstrations, although Hue and Danang still remained in rebel hands. Then Ky, without warning, broke the fragile truce by announcing that it would take at least a year or more to organize the elections, and that he intended to stay in power in the meantime. United States officials tried to water down the effect of the premier's statement by saying that it didn't mean what it seemed to mean, and the elections would be held in any case. But Ky's foes were sure they knew exactly what he did mean, and the rumblings of revolt sounded again.

This time Ky did not parley. In the middle of May, six battalions of his elite troops—paratroopers, marines and rangers—invaded Danang. When Thi's soldiers resisted, the battle was on. It raged in the streets and in the pagodas which the defenders had turned into fortresses. Government planes hit enemy positions with rockets and cannon fire; tanks poured shells into Buddhist temples. The fighting lasted eight days. Then the rebels surrendered. But it was an uneasy triumph for Ky, as victory was followed by a new outbreak of fiery Buddhist suicides.

Crisis-ridden South Vietnam still teetered perilously close to civil strife.

The puzzled, agitated Americans looked around at the shambles and asked themselves where they had gone wrong. Would the rural war against the Viet Cong be lost in the riot-torn cities? That would be the greatest irony of all. Why, after twelve years of costly effort, was there still no stable government in South Vietnam? The present turmoil was subsiding, but what hope was there for the future in this land of crisis without end? When would a new crisis come? And would the next one, perhaps, prove fatal?

They could truly wonder.

Was this war—so different—so irritating—so much beyond control—really worth fighting?

Would all of Asia really fall to communism if South Vietnam went down, as the domino theory said it would?

Or was this conflict, as its opponents claimed, "the wrong war, at the wrong place, at the wrong time"—a mistake from beginning to end?

The French had once held this prickly nettle and then let go. Now the Americans had it, and the stings were getting poisonous. Would they hold on to it, no matter what, or would they, in the end, be forced to drop it, too? Only history would write the answer to that question.

One thing was certain. Vietnam, which had fought and bled for more than two thousand years, would still be there when the fighting was over. The patient peasant, bound to the soil and the seasons, would still go out to work in the rice paddies where the seeds of life were growing. And as long as this was true, life would win out over death. For that, in the long run, has been the story of Vietnam.

INDEX

ANNAM, 52–55, 76
Argenlieu, Admiral d', 86, 88
Asia, 33, 36, 67–68, 73, 96–98

BA CUT, 107
Ball, George W., 164
Banks and banking, 59, 61
Bao Dai, Emperor, 84, 88, 98–
    100, 104–105, 107, 109
Bay Vien, 104–105, 106
Binh Xuyen, 104–107
Blum, Leon, 87–88
Bombing of North Vietnam,
    151–152, 153, 155, 160–161,
    162–164
Bonard, Admiral, 44
Browne, Malcolm, 134, 141
Buddhist sects, 105–106, 139–
    142, 166–167
Bundy, McGeorge, 164
Burma, 81, 96

CAM RANH BAY, 159
Cambodia, 23, 43, 54, 76, 107,
    149
Can Lao or Personalist Labor
    Revolutionary Party, 108,
    111, 127
Can Vuong or Monarchist Move-
    ment, 63
Cao Dai, 104, 105–107
Capitalism, 32, 68
Catholics, 139–140, 148, 157
    missionaries, 26–30, 35, 36, 38–
        40, 43
    persecution of, 35, 38–40, 41,
        43
Catroux, General Georges, 81
Central Vietnam, 109, 137–138,
    147
Cham empire, 22–23
Chasseloup-Laubat, 42, 46
Chiang Kai-shek, 74–75, 81, 82–
    83, 85, 89, 91, 98

China, 36–37, 42, 46–47, 73–75,
    89–90
    emigrants to Vietnam, 59
    invasion of Vietnam, 17–22,
        34, 54
    Kuomintang party, 65, 73–75,
        89
    Opium War, 37
Chinese Communists, 97–98, 101,
    155, 164
Chinese Nationalists, 98
Cholon, 104–105, 145
Chu Lai, 158–159
Civil Guard, 110, 119
Climate, 41–42, 44
Cochinchina, 25, 27–30, 70, 86
    French conquest of, 27–30, 40,
        54–56
Collins, Gen. J. Lawton, 104, 106
Colonialism, 36, 51, 59, 96–97
Communism, 14, 62, 67–79, 108
    China, 72–75, 89–90, 96–98,
        101, 155, 164
    expansion of, 97–99
    front groups, 74, 119
    historical development, 68–69,
        72–73
    Indochina, 74–79
    insurgency, 144, 117, 118
    propaganda, 69, 111, 114, 124
    subversion, 97, 114, 116, 121–
        122
    terror and violence, 114, 116,
        118, 119
Confucianism, 24, 57–58, 61, 63
Conway, Governor, 29–30
Counter-insurgency, 114, 152
Culture, 18–19, 56

DANANG, 153–154, 158, 166–167
De la Grandière, Admiral, 44–45
Democratic Republic of Viet-
    nam; see North Vietnam, 102
Diem; see Ngo Dinh Diem
Dienbienphu, fall of, 92–94, 97,
    98, 117
Dinh Bo Linh, Emperor, 22
Diseases, 41, 42, 44, 58

"Domino" theory, 98, 167
Dong Du or Pan-Asian Movement, 64, 75
Dong Hoi, 152
Dong Kinh Nghia Phuc or "Private Schools" Movement, 63
Dong Xoai, 158
Doumer, Governor-General Paul, 56
Dulles, John Foster, 97, 101
Duong Van Minh, 143, 145, 148
Dupré, Admiral, 46, 48–51
Dupuis, Jean, 47–51
Durbrow, Elbridge, 120, 130, 131
Dutch East Indies, 81, 96
Dutch traders, 25–26, 36, 39

ECONOMY, 56, 58, 59, 101, 148
U.S. aid, 110, 125, 143, 153
Education, 19, 24, 56–58, 63–64
Eisenhower, Dwight David, 95, 98, 104, 106, 152
Elections, 107, 109, 166
reunification, 102, 104, 109, 111
Emperor, role of, 24, 57, 63
Europeans, 37–40
colonies, 24–40, 96
Vietnamese fear of, 30, 34–36, 38, 53

FALL, BERNARD, 14, 118
Famines, 76
Farms and farming, 18–19, 23, 32–33, 58, 60
Felt, Admiral Harry D., 134
Ferry, Jules, 52
Feudal lords, 18–20, 23
France, 27–31, 33–71, 99, 101, 167
anti-French feelings, 45–46
civil servants, 45, 57, 62
colonial expansion, 13, 14, 27–31, 34, 36–37, 39–40, 41–66, 77, 154
Indochina War, 80–95
missionaries, 26–31
protectorates, 52–54
World War II, 80
Freedom, Vietnamese love of, 21, 53, 54, 108
French Revolution, 30, 58
Fulbright, J. William, 163

GARNIER, FRANCIS, 46–51

Gavin, Gen. James M., 163–164
Geneva Conference, 92, 96–97, 99, 101–103, 109
Genouilly, Admiral Rigualt de, 40, 42
Gia Long, Emperor, 30, 33–36
Giap, General; see Vo Nguyen Giap
Gracey, General Douglas, 85
Great Britain, 25, 33, 36–38, 39, 85, 96
Green Berets, 158, 159
Guerrilla warfare, 45, 83, 110, 112, 113–125, 148
communist approach, 116
historical development, 114–116
nature of, 113–114
support of the people, 113, 117–118
Guizot, François, 37, 39
Gulf of Tonkin incident, 150–151

HAIPHONG, 86, 87
Ham Nghi, Emperor, 56
Hanoi, North Vietnam, 27, 52, 65, 86, 88, 91, 103
captured by Viet Minh, 84
seizure by Dupuis, 47–51
University of, 64
Harbors and ports, 19, 58
Harkins, General Paul D., 133, 150
History of Vietnam, 13, 14–40
ancient beginnings, 13, 17–18
civil war between Trinh and Nguyen, 23–24, 25
early Chinese invasions, 18–22
European traders, 25–40
expansionist drive, 22–23
Ho Chi Minh, 62, 66, 67–79, 85, 100, 102, 133, 143, 153, 156, 161
aliases, 67, 69, 71, 73, 82
communist training, 69, 73–79, 83
early life, 69–74
leader of Viet Minh, 82–83, 103
negotiations with France, 86–88
president of Vietnam, 85
Ho Chi Minh Trail, 123, 149
Hoa Hao, 104, 105–107
Hong Kong, 37, 75, 76, 78

Honolulu Conference, 164–166
Hue, 48–49, 51, 55, 57, 158, 166
  Buddhist rebellion, 140–141
Huynh Phu So, 105

IMPERIALISM, 45–46
India, 25, 29, 36, 62, 88, 96
Indochina, 54–66, 80–95
  communism, 66, 74–77, 79, 90
  end of French empire, 80–95
  French rule, 54–66, 80–84, 85–
    86
  Japanese occupation, 81–85
  Viet Minh, 84–95
Indochinese Union, 54
Indonesia, 96
Industrial development, 58–61
Industrial Revolution, effects of,
  32–33, 51–52
Infiltration from the North, 122–
  123, 125, 137, 149, 152–153,
  160, 161–162
Isolation, policy of, 34, 35–36,
  38, 56

JAPAN, 36, 52, 81–85
Johnson, Lyndon B., 147, 151–
  152, 154, 155–156, 158
  Honolulu Conference, 164–166
  peace offers, 156, 160–162
  trip to Saigon, 132
Johnson, U. Alexis, 150
Jungle fighting, 138

KENNAN, GEORGE F., 163
Kennedy, John F., 100, 129–130,
  131–133, 141, 143, 146–147,
  152
Khanh, General; see Nguyen
  Khanh
Khmer Empire, Cambodia, 23
Korean war, 92, 95–96, 98, 110
Ky, Marshal; see Nguyen Cao
  Ky

LABOR UNIONS, 62, 76
Lagrée, Capt. Doudart de, 46
Lam Duc Thu, 75
Land reforms, 27, 90, 111, 117,
  119, 123
Landowners, 20, 59–60, 76–77
Language and writing, 19, 26, 58
Lansdale, General Edward, 129
Lao Dong (Communist Party),
  90, 122

Laos, 55, 77, 93, 132, 137, 149
  routes through, 123, 160
Lawrence, Colonel T. F. (Law-
  rence of Arabia), 116
Le Duan, 122, 123
Le dynasty, 23, 28, 43
Le Van Kim, 143
Leclerc, General Philippe, 85
Lenin, Vladimir Ilyich, 69, 72
Lien Viet, 87
Lodge, Henry Cabot, 141–142,
  144–145, 150, 164, 166
Ly Bon, 20

MA TUYEN, 145
McNamara, Robert S., 134, 149
Malaya, 81, 96, 117, 129
Mandarins, 24, 34–35, 56, 57–
  58, 61, 63
  decline in influence, 43–44, 57–
    58
Mao Tse-tung, 78, 82–83, 89–90,
  98, 133
  aid to Viet Minh, 90
  war strategy, 91, 94, 117–118,
    120
Mekong River, 43, 46–47, 49, 107
Millet, Stanley, 135
Mineral resources, 58–59, 81
Minh, General; see Duong Van
  Minh
Minh Mang, Emperor, 30, 35,
  38
Missionaries, 26–30, 35, 36, 38–
  40, 43
Mobile warfare, 91–92, 152–153,
  157–158
Molotov, Vlachislav M., 102
Montagnards, 137–138
Morse, Wayne, 163
Mosby, John S., 115
Mountains, 18, 137–138
Myers, Gen. Samuel L., 120

NAPOLEON, 33, 45–46, 114
Napoleon III, 39–40, 42, 45
National Assembly, 108, 127
National Liberation Committee,
  84
National Liberation Front, 122,
  124, 161
Nationalism, 61, 68, 88, 98
  movements, 14, 61, 62–66, 73,
    76, 82, 83, 87
Nationalist Party of Vietnam, 64–
  66, 76

Navarre, General Henri, 92
Ngo Dinh Can, 109, 147
Ngo Dinh Diem, 71, 88, 99–112,
    126–145
    character of, 126–127, 130–
    131, 132
    dictatorial measures, 108, 109–
    111, 118, 130–132
    leadership of, 107–108, 126,
    130, 146
    personal story, 99–101
    plots and coups against, 128–
    129, 131, 134–135, 138–139,
    143–145
    political opposition to, 103–
    112, 126, 128, 138
    struggle with Viet Cong, 122,
    125
    surrender and death of, 144–
    145, 147
    U.S. support of, 98, 100–102,
    106, 109–110, 112, 129–135,
    141, 143, 146
Ngo Dinh family, 100–101, 108,
    125, 127–128, 131, 138
Ngo Dinh Khoi, 100
Ngo Dinh Luyen, 109, 147
Ngo Dinh Nhu, 107–109, 125,
    127, 129, 130, 133, 135, 139,
    141–142, 143
    secret police, 127, 135, 142,
    147
Ngo Dinh Nhu, Madame, 108,
    131, 135, 139, 141, 142–143,
    147
Ngo Dinh Thuc, Archbishop,
    109, 140, 147
Ngo Quyen, General, 21
Ngo Van Chieu, 105
Nguyen Ai Quoc, 73, 82; see
    also Ho Chi Minh
Nguyen Anh, Prince, 28–30
Nguyen Cao Ky, Marshal, 157,
    164–167
    meeting with President John-
    son, 164–165
Nguyen Chan Thi, General, 165–
    167
Nguyen clan, 23–24, 25, 28
Nguyen Huu Tho, 123
Nguyen Khanh, General, 148–
    150, 156
Nguyen Ngoc Tho, 148
Nguyen Sin Huy, 70
Nguyen Thai Hoc, 64–65
Nguyen Van Hinh, General, 104

Nguyen Van Thieu, 164
Nguyen Van Trinh, 87
Nguyen Xuan Oanh, 149
Nhung, Captain, 145
Nolting, Frederick E., 130, 131,
    133, 141
North Atlantic Treaty Organi-
    zation (NATO), 97
North Vietnam, 23–24, 102–103,
    109, 152–153
    aid to Viet Cong; see Viet
    Cong
    communism, 14, 67–79, 111
    demand for elections, 109
    land reform, 111

PACIFICATION PROGRAMS, 110,
    152, 165
Peace, offer to negotiate, 155–
    157, 160–161
Peasants, 20–21, 23–24, 27, 43,
    60–61, 117–119, 167–168
    aid to Viet Cong, 117–119
    daily life, 24, 60–61
    hatred of French, 43, 45
    revolt by, 76–77
    southern and northern, 23–24
Pellerin, Bishop, 41
Pétain, Marshal Henri Philippe,
    80
People's Liberation Army, 122,
    124
Pham Van Dong, Premier, 70, 86
Phan Boi Chau, 64, 75
Phan Cong Tac, 107
Phan Huy Quat, Dr., 156–157
Phan Quang Dan, 127–128
Philastre, Monsieur, 51
Philippines, 25, 37, 62, 81, 129
Pigneau de Behaine, Bishop, 27–
    30, 33–35
Plei Me, 159
Pleiku, airbase at, 151
Police and courts, 62, 104, 108
    secret police, 127, 135, 142, 147
Political parties, 62–68
Portuguese traders, 24–27
Poulo Condore Island, 43, 65,
    128

QUINHON, 152
Quoc Ngu (system of writing),
    26

RABORN, VICE-ADMIRAL WIL-
    LIAM, 162

172

Radford, Admiral Arthur, 120
Railroads, 58, 59, 81, 89, 103
Red China; see Chinese Communists
Red River, 17–18, 47–50, 83, 84
Refugees, migration of, 103
Religious sects, 104, 105–107; see also Buddhist sects; Catholics
Rhodes, Monsignor Alexander of, 26–27
Rice, 19, 42, 43, 58, 59–60, 81, 89, 148, 168
Rivière, Captain Henri, 52
Roads and roadbuilding, 19, 58, 59, 89, 103
Rusk, Dean, 161, 163, 164
Russia, 39, 52; see also Soviet Union

SAIGON, 42–43, 48, 58, 77, 85, 87, 90, 103, 105–107, 147–148
crime and corruption, 104, 106
U.S. forces, 133–136
Self-Defense Corps, 110, 119
17th parallel, 23–24, 102, 107, 123, 152
Social conditions, 24, 56–61
Socialism, 68–69, 72
South Korean forces, 159
South Vietnam, 23–24, 70, 102, 107–108
American commitment, 132–133, 146, 150–152, 154–155
army, 127, 138–139, 149, 152
attack on Viet Cong, 111–112
casualty figures, 136
constitution, 108
economy, 148
instability of governments, 146–149, 156–157
opinion of U.S., 128
religious problems, 103, 105–107, 139–142, 166–167
Southeast Asia, 17, 98, 156
Southeast Asia Treaty Organization (SEATO), 97
Soviet Union, 96–97, 102, 154
communism, 69, 72–73
Spanish explorers, 25, 37, 39
Stalin, Joseph, 73, 78
Student demonstrations, 142, 148
Sun Yat Sen, 64, 65

TAY SON REBELLION, 28–30, 34–35

Taylor, General Maxwell, 132, 150, 163
Thailand, 29, 36, 76
Than Van Huong, 149
Thich Quang Duc, 141
Thich Tri Quang, 165–166
Thieu Au, 20
Thieu Tri, 35, 38
Ton That Dinh, 144–145
Tonking, 41, 54–55
French occupation, 41, 48, 50–55
Tourane, 40, 41, 45
Tran Trong Kim, 84
Tran Van Chuong, 131
Tran Van Do, 102
Tran Van Don, General, 143
Tran Van Giau, 85
Trieu Da, General, 17–18
Trinh, rule of, 23, 25, 28
Trotsky, Leon, 73
Trung sisters, 19
Tu Duc, Emperor, 35, 38, 42, 43–44, 47–49, 52–53

UNITED STATES IN VIETNAM, 13, 96–99, 101–102, 120, 146–168
anti-war sentiment, 120, 154–155, 162–164
commitment to South Vietnam, 132–133, 146–147, 151
economic and military aid, 92, 110, 125, 143, 154–155, 156
forces in Vietnam, 133, 137, 146, 152–154, 158–160
peace offensive, 156, 161

VIET CONG, 111–112, 124, 161
casualties, 149, 159–160
guerrilla warfare, 113–125
infiltrators from North, 122–123, 124, 137, 149, 152–153, 160, 162
mobile warfare, 90–92, 153, 157
monsoon offensives, 149–150, 157, 160
terror and violence, 111–112, 114, 116, 118, 119–122, 124
Viet Minh, 81–95, 118, 121
founding of, 82–83
guerrilla actions, 82–83, 85–89, 90–91
Indochina War, 83–95

173

Vietnam; *see also* North Vietnam; South Vietnam
  division of, 23–24, 55, 102
  independence of, 36, 64, 85, 88, 99
Vietnam War, 146–168
  American intervention, 132–133, 146, 150–151, 153–154
  casualties, 149, 160
  escalation, 153
  infiltration, 122–123, 125, 137, 149, 153, 160, 162
  peace offensive, 156, 161
Vietnamese, 17–18, 23–24, 137–138
  anti-American feelings, 154, 165

Villages, 59–61, 110–111, 165
  education, 58
  murders of chiefs, 121
  Viet Cong controlled, 119, 123–124, 136–137
Vinh Yen, battle at, 91, 92
VNQDD (Viet-Nam Quoc-Dan Dang), 65, 76
Vo Nguyen Giap, 70, 82–83, 88–89, 90–95, 117, 137

WESTERN IDEAS, impact of, 56–58, 63–64
Westmoreland, Gen. William C., 150, 158–159

YEN BAY UPRISING, 65, 76